THE
ADVENT
OF DIVINE
JUSTICE

By Shoghi Effendi
God Passes By
The Promised Day Is Come

Collections of Letters and Messages
Bahá'í Administration
This Decisive Hour
Citadel of Faith
Messages to the Bahá'í World
The World Order of Bahá'u'lláh

Translations
The Dawn-Breakers
Epistle to the Son of the Wolf
Gleanings from the Writings of Bahá'u'lláh
The Hidden Words
The Kitáb-i-Íqán
Prayers and Meditations

THE
ADVENT
OF DIVINE
JUSTICE

by
Shoghi Effendi

BAHÁ'Í
PUBLISHING TRUST

WILMETTE, ILLINOIS

Bahá'í Publishing Trust, Wilmette, Illinois 60091-2844

Copyright 1939, © 1963, 1967, 1984, 1990, 2006
by the National Spiritual Assembly
of the Bahá'ís of the United States
All rights reserved. Published 2006
Printed in the United States of America

20 19 18   6 5 4

New pocket-size edition 2006

Library of Congress Cataloging-in-Publication Data

Shoghi, Effendi.
    The advent of divine justice / by Shoghi Effendi.— New ed.
      p. cm.
    Includes index.
    ISBN-13: 978-0-87743-321-7 (alk. paper)
    ISBN-10: 0-87743-321-6 (alk. paper)
    1. Bahai Faith—North America—Miscellanea. 2. Shoghi,
Effendi—Correspondence. I. Title.

BP364.A57 2006
297.9'386—dc22

                                        2005057199

Cover design by John Solarz

CONTENTS

With the approval of the Universal House of Justice the editors eliminated the subheadings added to the first edition of *The Advent of Divine Justice* in 1939 and have, instead, prepared a table of contents based on the principle of identifying themes, section by section, that appear in the book.

CONTENTS

CONTENTS

PREFACE

From the earliest years of his ministry as the divinely appointed Guardian of the Cause of God, Shoghi Effendi conferred upon the Bahá'ís of North America a very special bounty in addressing to them a series of inspiring and challenging messages, carefully delineating the tasks they were called upon to discharge, and emphasizing the relationship of these goals to the fulfillment of their destiny as the chosen instruments for the execution of the Divine Plan of 'Abdu'l-Bahá.

Of all these communications, perhaps the one most directly related to the life of the individual Bahá'í was *The Advent of Divine Justice,* written in 1938, in which the Guardian set forth the spiritual prerequisites for success in every activity for the advancement of the Faith. Special emphasis was placed not only upon the imponderable factors associated with the inner life of the spirit, but also upon the human and social relationships which must be cultivated and made an integral part of the daily life of every Bahá'í.

Describing with amazing accuracy the basic ills afflicting the American body politic, as well as indicating the probable course of world events which were destined to create new challenges and opportunities for the American nation, Shoghi Effendi in this portentous message clearly defined the role the American Bahá'ís would be called upon to play in the years ahead.

At this time, when so many of the prophetic utterances of both 'Abdu'l-Bahá and Shoghi Effendi relating to America have a deeper meaning and significance than ever before in their impact on the activities of the American believers, it is particularly befitting that a new edition of *The Advent of Divine Justice* be made available, providing the opportunity for every Bahá'í to glean from a careful study of its pages a clearer understanding of the true purpose of our Faith, of America's spiritual destiny, and of the manner in which the individual believer is called upon to contribute to the achievement of this destiny, both on the homefront and in foreign fields of service.

—Paul Haney

Bahá'í World Center
Haifa, Israel
November 1968

THE
ADVENT
OF
DIVINE
JUSTICE

■■■
■■■
■■■

Was written shortly after the launch
of the 7 year plan.
Its saying you are doing a good job.
Saying to so pioneering

THE ADVENT OF DIVINE JUSTICE

To the beloved of God and the handmaids of the Merciful throughout the United States and Canada.

Best-beloved brothers and sisters
in the love of Bahá'u'lláh:

It would be difficult indeed to adequately express the feelings of irrepressible joy and exultation that flood my heart every time I pause to contemplate the ceaseless evidences of the dynamic energy which animates the stalwart pioneers of the World Order of Bahá'u'lláh in the execution of the Plan committed to their charge. The signature of the contract, by your elected national representatives, signalizing the opening of the final phase of the greatest enterprise ever launched by the followers of the Faith of Bahá'u'lláh in the West, no less than the extremely heartening progress recorded in the successive reports of their National Teaching Committee, attest, beyond the shadow of a doubt, the

1

fidelity, the vigor, and the thoroughness with which you are conducting the manifold operations which the evolution of the Seven Year Plan must necessarily involve. In both of its aspects, and in all its details, it is being prosecuted with exemplary regularity and precision, with undiminished efficiency, and commendable dispatch.

2   The resourcefulness which the national representatives of the American believers have, in recent months, so strikingly demonstrated, as evidenced by the successive measures they have adopted, has been matched by the loyal, the unquestioning and generous support accorded them by all those whom they represent, at every critical stage, and with every fresh advance, in the discharge of their sacred duties. Such close interaction, such complete cohesion, such continual harmony and fellowship between the various agencies that contribute to the organic life, and constitute the basic framework, of every properly functioning Bahá'í community, is a phenomenon which offers a striking contrast to the disruptive tendencies which the discordant elements of present-day society so tragically manifest. Whereas every apparent trial with which the unfathomable wisdom of the Almighty deems it necessary to afflict His chosen community serves only to demonstrate afresh its essential solidarity and to consolidate its inward strength, each of the successive crises in the

This pre world war II but when Hitler was in power.

fortunes of a decadent age exposes more convincingly than the one preceding it the corrosive influences that are fast sapping the vitality and undermining the basis of its declining institutions. *Health care, global corruption politics....*

For such demonstrations of the interpositions of an ever-watchful Providence *Good fortune from God.* they who stand identified *Force that intervens.* with the Community of the Most Great Name must feel eternally grateful. From every fresh token of His unfailing blessing on the one hand, and of His visitation on the other, they cannot but derive immense hope and courage. Alert to seize every opportunity which the revolutions of the wheel of destiny within their Faith offers them, and undismayed by the prospect of spasmodic convulsions *Labor pains* that must sooner or later fatally affect those who have refused to embrace its light, they, and those who will labor after them, must press forward until the processes now set in motion will have each spent its force and contributed its share towards the birth of the Order now stirring in the womb of a travailing age.

These recurrent crises which, with ominous frequency and resistless force, are afflicting an ever-increasing portion of the human race must of necessity continue, however impermanently, to exercise, in a certain measure, their baleful influence upon a world community which has spread its ramifications to the uttermost ends of the earth. How can the beginnings of a world

4

How could all this upheaval not effect the faith. right after war

upheaval, unleashing forces that are so gravely derang-
ing the social, the religious, the political, and the economic equilibrium of organized society, throwing into
chaos and confusion political systems, racial doctrines,
social conceptions, cultural standards, religious associations, and trade relationships—how can such agita-
tions, on a scale so vast, so unprecedented, fail to produce any repercussions on the institutions of a Faith of
such tender age whose teachings have a direct and vital
bearing on each of these spheres of human life and
conduct?

5   Little wonder, therefore, if they who are holding aloft
the banner of so pervasive a Faith, so challenging a
Cause, find themselves affected by the impact of these
world-shaking forces. Little wonder if they find that in
the midst of this whirlpool of contending passions their
freedom has been curtailed, their tenets contemned,
their institutions assaulted, their motives maligned,
their authority jeopardized, their claim rejected.

6   In the heart of the European continent a community which, as predicted by 'Abdu'l-Bahá, is destined,
by virtue of its spiritual potentialities and geographical situation, to radiate the splendor of the light of
the Faith on the countries that surround it, has been
momentarily eclipsed through the restrictions which a
regime that has sorely misapprehended its purpose and
function has chosen to impose upon it. Its voice, alas,

[handwritten margin note: The Bahai institutions are rejected. Bahais are condemned.]

[handwritten interlineation: believe]

[handwritten note at bottom: Hitler was doing a cleansing. Stoped the NSA & all activities.]

is now silenced, its institutions dissolved, its literature banned, its archives confiscated, and its meetings suspended.

In central Asia, in the city enjoying the unique distinction of having been chosen by 'Abdu'l-Bahá as the home of the first Mashriqu'l-Adhkár of the Bahá'í world, as well as in the towns and villages of the province to which it belongs, the sore-pressed Faith of Bahá'u'lláh, as a result of the extraordinary and unique vitality which, in the course of several decades, it has consistently manifested, finds itself at the mercy of forces which, alarmed at its rising power, are now bent on reducing it to utter impotence. Its Temple, though still used for purposes of Bahá'í worship, has been expropriated, its Assemblies and committees disbanded, its teaching activities crippled, its chief promoters deported, and not a few of its most enthusiastic supporters, both men and women, imprisoned.

In the land of its birth, wherein reside the immense majority of its followers—a country whose capital has been hailed by Bahá'u'lláh as the *"mother of the world"* and the *"dayspring of the joy of mankind"*—a civil authority, as yet undivorced officially from the paralyzing influences of an antiquated, a fanatical, and outrageously corrupt clergy, pursues relentlessly its campaign of repression against the adherents of a Faith which it has for well-nigh a century striven unsuccessfully to

This is Eshghabad

7

8

5

suppress. Indifferent to the truth that the members of this innocent and proscribed community can justly claim to rank as among the most disinterested, the most competent, and the most ardent lovers of their native land, contemptuous of their high sense of world citizenship which the advocates of an excessive and narrow nationalism can never hope to appreciate, such an authority refuses to grant to a Faith which extends its spiritual jurisdiction over well-nigh six hundred local communities, and which numerically outnumbers the adherents of either the Christian, the Jewish, or the Zoroastrian Faiths in that land, the necessary legal right to enforce its laws, to administer its affairs, to conduct its schools, to celebrate its festivals, to circulate its literature, to solemnize its rites, to erect its edifices, and to safeguard its endowments.

9   And now recently in the Holy Land itself, the heart and nerve-center of a world-embracing Faith, the fires of racial animosity, of fratricidal strife, of unabashed terrorism, have lit a conflagration that gravely interferes, on the one hand, with that flow of pilgrims that constitutes the lifeblood of that center, and suspends, on the other, the various projects that had been initiated in connection with the preservation and extension of the areas surrounding the sacred Spots it enshrines. The safety of the small community of resident believers, faced by the rising tide of lawlessness, has

been imperiled, its status as a neutral and distinct community indirectly challenged, and its freedom to carry out certain of its observances curtailed. A series of murderous assaults, alternating with outbursts of bitter fanaticism, both racial and religious, involving the leaders as well as the followers of the three leading Faiths in that distracted country, have, at times, threatened to sever all normal communications both within its confines as well as with the outside world. Perilous though the situation has been, the Bahá'í Holy Places, the object of the adoration of a world-encircling Faith, have, notwithstanding their number and exposed position, and though to outward seeming deprived of any means of protection, been vouchsafed a preservation little short of miraculous.

A world, torn with conflicting passions, and perilously disintegrating from within, finds itself confronted, at so crucial an epoch in its history, by the rising fortunes of an infant Faith, a Faith that, at times, seems to be drawn into its controversies, entangled by its conflicts, eclipsed by its gathering shadows, and overpowered by the mounting tide of its passions. In its very heart, within its cradle, at the seat of its first and venerable Temple, in one of its hitherto flourishing and potentially powerful centers, the as-yet unemancipated Faith of Bahá'u'lláh seems indeed to have retreated before the onrushing forces of violence and disorder to which humanity is steadily falling a victim. The strong-holds of such a Faith, one by one and day after day, are to outward seeming being successively isolated, as-saulted and captured. As the lights of liberty flicker and go out, as the din of discord grows louder and louder every day, as the fires of fanaticism flame with increasing fierceness in the breasts of men, as the chill of irreligion creeps relentlessly over the soul of man-kind, the limbs and organs that constitute the body of the Faith of Bahá'u'lláh appear, in varying measure, to have become afflicted with the crippling influences that now hold in their grip the whole of the civilized world.

11   How clearly and strikingly the following words of 'Abdu'l-Bahá are being demonstrated at this hour: *"The darkness of error that has enveloped the East and the West is, in this most great cycle, battling with the light of Divine Guidance. Its swords and its spears are very sharp and pointed; its army keenly bloodthirsty." "This day,"* He, in another passage has written, *"the powers of all the leaders of religion are directed towards the dispersion of the congregation of the All-Merciful, and the shattering of the Divine Edifice. The hosts of the world, whether material, cultural or political are from every side launch-ing their assault, for the Cause is great, very great. Its great-ness is, in this day, clear and manifest to men's eyes."*

12   The one chief remaining citadel, the mighty arm which still raises aloft the standard of an unconquer-

able Faith, is none other than the blessed community of the followers of the Most Great Name in the North American continent. By its works, and through the unfailing protection vouchsafed to it by an almighty Providence, this distinguished member of the body of the constantly interacting Bahá'í communities of East and West, bids fair to be universally regarded as the cradle, as well as the stronghold, of that future New World Order, which is at once the promise and the glory of the Dispensation associated with the name of Bahá'u'lláh.

Let anyone inclined to either belittle the unique station conferred upon this community, or to question the role it will be called upon to play in the days to come, ponder the implication of these pregnant and highly illuminating words uttered by 'Abdu'l-Bahá, and addressed to it at a time when the fortunes of a world groaning beneath the burden of a devastating war had reached their lowest ebb. *"The continent of America,"* He so significantly wrote, *"is, in the eyes of the one true God, the land wherein the splendors of His light shall be revealed, where the mysteries of His Faith shall be unveiled, where the righteous will abide, and the free assemble."*

Already, the community of the believers of the North American continent—at once the prime mover and pattern of the future communities which the Faith of

Bahá'u'lláh is destined to raise up throughout the length and breadth of the Western Hemisphere—has, despite the prevailing gloom, shown its capacity to be recognized as the torchbearer of that light, the repository of those mysteries, the exponent of that righteousness and the sanctuary of that freedom. To what other light can these above-quoted words possibly allude, if not to the light of the glory of the Golden Age of the Faith of Bahá'u'lláh? What mysteries could 'Abdu'l-Bahá have contemplated except the mysteries of that embryonic World Order now evolving within the matrix of His Administration? What righteousness if not the righteousness whose reign that Age and that Order can alone establish? What freedom but the freedom which the proclamation of His sovereignty in the fullness of time must bestow?

15   The community of the organized promoters of the Faith of Bahá'u'lláh in the American continent—the spiritual descendants of the dawn-breakers of an heroic Age, who by their death proclaimed the birth of that Faith—must, in turn, usher in, not by their death but through living sacrifice, that promised World Order, the shell ordained to enshrine that priceless jewel, the world civilization, of which the Faith itself is the sole begetter. While its sister communities are bending beneath the tempestuous winds that beat upon them from every side, this community, preserved by the im-

mutable decrees of the omnipotent Ordainer and deriving continual sustenance from the mandate with which the Tablets of the Divine Plan have invested it, is now busily engaged in laying the foundations and in fostering the growth of those institutions which are to herald the approach of the Age destined to witness the birth and rise of the World Order of Bahá'u'lláh.

A community, relatively negligible in its numerical 16 strength; separated by vast distances from both the focal-center of its Faith and the land wherein the preponderating mass of its fellow-believers reside; bereft in the main of material resources and lacking in experience and in prominence; ignorant of the beliefs, concepts and habits of those peoples and races from which its spiritual Founders have sprung; wholly unfamiliar with the languages in which its sacred Books were originally revealed; constrained to place its sole reliance upon an inadequate rendering of only a fragmentary portion of the literature embodying its laws, its tenets, and its history; subjected from its infancy to tests of extreme severity, involving, at times, the defection of some of its most prominent members; having to contend, ever since its inception, and in an ever-increasing measure, with the forces of corruption, of moral laxity, and ingrained prejudice—such a community, in less than half a century, and unaided by any of its sister communities, whether in the East or in the West, has, by virtue of the celestial potency with which an all-loving Master has abundantly endowed it, lent an impetus to the onward march of the Cause it has espoused which the combined achievements of its coreligionists in the West have failed to rival.

17   What other community, it can confidently be asked, has been instrumental in fixing the pattern, and in imparting the original impulse, to those administrative institutions that constitute the vanguard of the World Order of Bahá'u'lláh? What other community has been capable of demonstrating, with such consistency, the resourcefulness, the discipline, the iron determination, the zeal and perseverance, the devotion and fidelity, so indispensable to the erection and the continued extension of the framework within which those nascent institutions can alone multiply and mature? What other community has proved itself to be fired by so noble a vision, or willing to rise to such heights of self-sacrifice, or ready to achieve so great a measure of solidarity, as to be able to raise, in so short a time and in the course of such crucial years, an edifice that can well deserve to be regarded as the greatest contribution ever made by the West to the Cause of Bahá'u'lláh? What other community can justifiably lay claim to have succeeded, through the unsupported efforts of one of its humble members, in securing the spontaneous allegiance of Royalty to its Cause, and in

winning such marvelous and written testimonies to its truth? What other community has shown the foresight, the organizing ability, the enthusiastic eagerness, that have been responsible for the establishment and multiplication, throughout its territory, of those initial schools which, as time goes by, will, on the one hand, evolve into powerful centers of Bahá'í learning, and, on the other, provide a fertile recruiting ground for the enrichment and consolidation of its teaching force? What other community has produced pioneers combining to such a degree the essential qualities of audacity, of consecration, of tenacity, of self-renunciation, and unstinted devotion, that have prompted them to abandon their homes, and forsake their all, and scatter over the surface of the globe, and hoist in its uttermost corners the triumphant banner of Bahá'u'lláh? Who else but the members of this community have won the eternal distinction of being the first to raise the call of *Yá Bahá'u'l-Abhá* in such highly important and widely scattered centers and territories as the hearts of both the British and French empires, Germany, the Far East, the Balkan States, the Scandinavian countries, Latin America, the Islands of the Pacific, South Africa, Australia and New Zealand, and now more recently the Baltic States? Who else but those same pioneers have shown themselves ready to undertake the labor, to exercise the patience, and to provide the funds, required for the translation and publication, in no less than forty languages, of their sacred literature, the dissemination of which is an essential prerequisite to any effectively organized campaign of teaching? What other community can lay claim to have had a decisive share in the worldwide efforts that have been exerted for the safeguarding and the extension of the immediate surroundings of its holy shrines, as well as for the preliminary acquisition of the future sites of its international institutions at its world center? What other community can to its eternal credit claim to have been the first to frame its national and local constitutions, thereby laying down the fundamental lines of the twin charters designed to regulate the activities, define the functions, and safeguard the rights, of its institutions? What other community can boast of having simultaneously acquired and legally secured the basis of its national endowments, thus paving the way for a similar action on the part of its local communities? What other community has achieved the supreme distinction of having obtained, long before any of its sister communities had envisaged such a possibility, the necessary documents assuring the recognition, by both the federal and state authorities, of its Spiritual Assemblies and national endowments? And finally what other community has had the privilege, and been granted the means, to succor the needy, to plead the cause of the downtrodden, and to intervene so energetically for the safeguarding of Bahá'í edifices and institutions in countries such as Persia, Egypt, 'Iráq, Russia, and Germany, where, at various times, its fellow-believers have had to suffer the rigors of both religious and racial persecution?

Such a matchless and brilliant record of service, extending over a period of well-nigh twenty years, and so closely interwoven with the interest and fortunes of such a large section of the worldwide Bahá'í community, deserves to rank as a memorable chapter in the history of the Formative Period of the Faith of Bahá'u'lláh. Reinforced and enriched as it is by the memory of the American believers' earlier achievements, such a record is in itself convincing testimony to their ability to befittingly shoulder the responsibilities which any task may impose upon them in the future. To overrate the significance of these manifold services would be well-nigh impossible. To appraise correctly their value, and dilate on their merits and immediate consequences, is a task which only a future Bahá'í historian can properly discharge. I can only for the present place on record my profound conviction that a community capable of showing forth such deeds, of evincing such a spirit, of rising to such heights, cannot but be already possessed of such potentialities as will enable it to vindicate, in

18

the fullness of time, its right to be acclaimed as the chief creator and champion of the World Order of Bahá'u'lláh.

19   Magnificent as has been this record, reminiscent as it is, in some of its aspects, of the exploits with which the dawn-breakers of an heroic Age have proclaimed the birth of the Faith itself, the task associated with the name of this privileged community is, far from approaching its climax, only beginning to unfold. What the American believers have, within the space of almost fifty years, achieved is infinitesimal when compared to the magnitude of the tasks ahead of them. The rumblings of that catastrophic upheaval, which is to proclaim, at one and the same time, the death-pangs of the old order and the birth-pangs of the new, indicate both the steady approach, as well as the awe-inspiring character, of those tasks.

20   The virtual establishment of the Administrative Order of their Faith, the erection of its framework, the fashioning of its instruments, and the consolidation of its subsidiary institutions, was the first task committed to their charge, as an organized community called into being by the Will, and under the instructions, of 'Abdu'l-Bahá. Of this initial task they have acquitted themselves with marvelous promptitude, fidelity, and vigor. No sooner had they created and correlated the various and necessary agencies for the efficient conduct

of any policy they might subsequently wish to initiate, than they addressed themselves, with equal zest and consecration, to the next more arduous task of erecting the superstructure of an edifice the cornerstone of which 'Abdu'l-Bahá Himself had laid. And when that feat was achieved, this community, alive to the passionate pleas, exhortations, and promises recorded in the Tablets of the Divine Plan, resolved to undertake yet another task, which in its scope and spiritual potentialities is sure to outshine any of the works they have already accomplished. Launching with unquenchable enthusiasm and dauntless courage the Seven Year Plan, as the first and practical step towards the fulfillment of the mission prescribed in those epoch-making Tablets, they entered, with a spirit of renewed consecration, upon their dual task, the consummation of which, it is hoped, will synchronize with the celebration of the centenary of the birth of the Faith of Bahá'u'lláh. Well aware that every advance made in the external ornamentation of their majestic edifice would directly react on the progress of the teaching campaign initiated by them in both the northern and southern American continents, and realizing that every victory gained in the teaching field would, in its turn, facilitate the work, and hasten the completion, of their Temple, they are now pressing on, with courage and faith, in their efforts to discharge, in both of its phases, their obligations under the Plan they have dedicated themselves to execute.

21   Let them not, however, imagine that the carrying out of the Seven Year Plan, coinciding as it does with the termination of the first century of the Bahá'í era, signifies either the termination of, or even an interruption in, the work which the unerring Hand of the Almighty is directing them to perform. The opening of the second century of the Bahá'í era must needs disclose greater vistas, usher in further stages, and witness the initiation of plans more far-reaching than any as yet conceived. The Plan on which is now focused the attention, the aspirations, and the resources of the entire community of the American believers should be viewed as a mere beginning, as a trial of strength, a stepping-stone to a crusade of still greater magnitude, if the duties and responsibilities with which the Author of the Divine Plan has invested them are to be honorably and entirely fulfilled.

22   For the consummation of the present Plan can result in no more than the formation of at least one center in each of the Republics of the Western Hemisphere, whereas the duties prescribed in those Tablets call for a wider diffusion, and imply the scattering of a far greater and more representative number of the members of the North American Bahá'í community over the entire surface of the New World. It is the undoubted mission

of the American believers, therefore, to carry forward into the second century the glorious work initiated in the closing years of the first. Not until they have played their part in guiding the activities of these isolated and newly fledged centers, and in fostering their capacity to initiate in their turn institutions, both local and national, modeled on their own, can they be satisfied to have adequately discharged their immediate obligations under 'Abdu'l-Bahá's divinely revealed Plan.

Nor should it for a moment be supposed that the completion of a task which aims at the multiplication of Bahá'í centers and the provision of the assistance and guidance necessary for the establishment of the Administrative Order of the Bahá'í Faith in the countries of Latin America realizes in its entirety the scheme visualized for them by 'Abdu'l-Bahá. A perusal, however perfunctory, of those Tablets embodying His Plan will instantly reveal a scope for their activities that stretches far beyond the confines of the Western Hemisphere. With their inter-American tasks and responsibilities virtually discharged, their intercontinental mission enters upon its most glorious and decisive phase. *"The moment this Divine Message,"* 'Abdu'l-Bahá Himself has written, *"is carried forward by the American believers from the shores of America and is propagated through the continents of Europe, of Asia, of Africa, and of Australasia, and as far as the islands of the Pacific, this* 23 *community will find itself securely established upon the throne of an everlasting dominion."*

24   And who knows but that when this colossal task has been accomplished a greater, a still more superb mission, incomparable in its splendor, and foreordained for them by Bahá'u'lláh, may not be thrust upon them? The glories of such a mission are of such dazzling splendor, the circumstances attending it so remote, and the contemporary events with the culmination of which it is so closely knit in such a state of flux, that it would be premature to attempt, at the present time, any accurate delineation of its features. Suffice it to say that out of the turmoil and tribulations of these "latter years" opportunities undreamt of will be born, and circumstances unpredictable created, that will enable, nay impel, the victorious prosecutors of 'Abdu'l-Bahá's Plan, to add, through the part they will play in the unrolling of the New World Order, fresh laurels to the crown of their servitude to the threshold of Bahá'u'lláh.

25   Nor should any of the manifold opportunities, of a totally different order, be allowed to pass unnoticed which the evolution of the Faith itself, whether at its world center, or in the North American continent, or even in the most outlying regions of the earth, must create, calling once again upon the American believers to play a part, no less conspicuous than the share they have previously had in their collective contributions to

the propagation of the Cause of Bahá'u'lláh. I can only for the moment cite at random certain of these opportunities which stand out preeminently, in any attempt to survey the possibilities of the future: The election of the International House of Justice and its establishment in the Holy Land, the spiritual and administrative center of the Bahá'í world, together with the formation of its auxiliary branches and subsidiary institutions; the gradual erection of the various dependencies of the first Mashriqu'l-Adhkár of the West, and the intricate issues involving the establishment and the extension of the structural basis of Bahá'í community life; the codification and promulgation of the ordinances of the Most Holy Book, necessitating the formation, in certain countries of the East, of properly constituted and officially recognized courts of Bahá'í law; the building of the third Mashriqu'l-Adhkár of the Bahá'í world in the outskirts of the city of Ṭihrán, to be followed by the rise of a similar House of Worship in the Holy Land itself; the deliverance of Bahá'í communities from the fetters of religious orthodoxy in such Islamic countries as Persia, 'Iráq, and Egypt, and the consequent recognition, by the civil authorities in those states, of the independent status and religious character of Bahá'í National and Local Assemblies; the precautionary and defensive measures to be devised, coordinated, and carried out to counteract the full force of the inescapable attacks which the organized efforts of ecclesiastical organizations of various denominations will progressively launch and relentlessly pursue; and, last but not least, the multitudinous issues that must be faced, the obstacles that must be overcome, and the responsibilities that must be assumed, to enable a sore-tried Faith to pass through the successive stages of unmitigated obscurity, of active repression, and of complete emancipation, leading in turn to its being acknowledged as an independent Faith, enjoying the status of full equality with its sister religions, to be followed by its establishment and recognition as a State religion, which in turn must give way to its assumption of the rights and prerogatives associated with the Bahá'í state, functioning in the plenitude of its powers, a stage which must ultimately culminate in the emergence of the worldwide Bahá'í Commonwealth, animated wholly by the spirit, and operating solely in direct conformity with the laws and principles of Bahá'u'lláh.

26   The challenge offered by these opportunities the American believers, I feel confident, will, in addition to their answer to the teaching call voiced by 'Abdu'l-Bahá in His Tablets, unhesitatingly take up, and will, with their traditional fearlessness, tenacity, and efficiency, so respond to it as to confirm, before all the world, their title and rank as the champion-builders of

the mightiest institutions of the Faith of Bahá'u'lláh.

Dearly beloved friends! Though the task be long and 27
arduous, yet the prize which the All-Bountiful Bestower
has chosen to confer upon you is of such preciousness
that neither tongue nor pen can befittingly appraise it.
Though the goal towards which you are now so strenu-
ously striving be distant, and as yet undisclosed to men's
eyes, yet its promise lies firmly embedded in the authoritative and unalterable utterances of Bahá'u'lláh.
Though the course He has traced for you seems, at
times, lost in the threatening shadows with which a
stricken humanity is now enveloped, yet the unfailing
light He has caused to shine continually upon you is
of such brightness that no earthly dusk can ever eclipse
its splendor. Though small in numbers, and circum-
scribed as yet in your experiences, powers, and resources, yet the Force which energizes your mission is
limitless in its range and incalculable in its potency.
Though the enemies which every acceleration in the
progress of your mission must raise up be fierce, numerous, and unrelenting, yet the invisible Hosts which,
if you persevere, must, as promised, rush forth to your
aid, will, in the end, enable you to vanquish their hopes
and annihilate their forces. Though the ultimate blessings that must crown the consummation of your mission be undoubted, and the Divine promises given you
firm and irrevocable, yet the measure of the goodly

reward which every one of you is to reap must depend on the extent to which your daily exertions will have contributed to the expansion of that mission and the hastening of its triumph.

28   Dearly beloved friends! Great as is my love and admiration for you, convinced as I am of the paramount share which you can, and will, undoubtedly have in both the continental and international spheres of future Bahá'í activity and service, I feel it nevertheless incumbent upon me to utter, at this juncture, a word of warning. The glowing tributes, so repeatedly and deservedly paid to the capacity, the spirit, the conduct, and the high rank, of the American believers, both individually and as an organic community, must, under no circumstances, be confounded with the characteristics and nature of the people from which God has raised them up. A sharp distinction between that community and that people must be made, and resolutely and fearlessly upheld, if we wish to give due recognition to the transmuting power of the Faith of Bahá'u'lláh, in its impact on the lives and standards of those who have chosen to enlist under His banner. Otherwise, the supreme and distinguishing function of His Revelation, which is none other than the calling into being of a new race of men, will remain wholly unrecognized and completely obscured.

How often have the Prophets of God, not except-
ing Bahá'u'lláh Himself, chosen to appear, and deliver
their Message in countries and amidst peoples and races,
at a time when they were either fast declining, or had
already touched the lowest depths of moral and spiritual degradation. The appalling misery and wretched-
ness to which the Israelites had sunk, under the debas-
ing and tyrannical rule of the Pharaohs, in the days
preceding their exodus from Egypt under the leader-
ship of Moses; the decline that had set in in the religious, the spiritual, the cultural, and the moral life of
the Jewish people, at the time of the appearance of
Jesus Christ; the barbarous cruelty, the gross idolatry
and immorality, which had for so long been the most
distressing features of the tribes of Arabia and brought
such shame upon them when Muḥammad arose to proclaim His Message in their midst; the indescribable state
of decadence, with its attendant corruption, confusion,
intolerance, and oppression, in both the civil and religious life of Persia, so graphically portrayed by the pen
of a considerable number of scholars, diplomats, and
travelers, at the hour of the Revelation of Bahá'u'lláh—
all demonstrate this basic and inescapable fact. To contend that the innate worthiness, the high moral standard, the political aptitude, and social attainments of
any race or nation is the reason for the appearance in
its midst of any of these Divine Luminaries would be

an absolute perversion of historical facts, and would amount to a complete repudiation of the undoubted interpretation placed upon them, so clearly and emphatically, by both Bahá'u'lláh and 'Abdu'l-Bahá.

30   How great, then, must be the challenge to those who, belonging to such races and nations, and having responded to the call which these Prophets have raised, to unreservedly recognize and courageously testify to this indubitable truth, that not by reason of any racial superiority, political capacity, or spiritual virtue which a race or nation might possess, but rather as a direct consequence of its crying needs, its lamentable degeneracy, and irremediable perversity, has the Prophet of God chosen to appear in its midst, and with it as a lever has lifted the entire human race to a higher and nobler plane of life and conduct. For it is precisely under such circumstances, and by such means that the Prophets have, from time immemorial, chosen and were able to demonstrate their redemptive power to raise from the depths of abasement and of misery, the people of their own race and nation, empowering them to transmit in turn to other races and nations the saving grace and the energizing influence of their Revelation.

31   In the light of this fundamental principle it should always be borne in mind, nor can it be sufficiently emphasized, that the primary reason why the Báb and Bahá'u'lláh chose to appear in Persia, and to make it

the first repository of their Revelation, was because, of all the peoples and nations of the civilized world, that race and nation had, as so often depicted by 'Abdu'l-Bahá, sunk to such ignominious depths, and manifested so great a perversity, as to find no parallel among its contemporaries. For no more convincing proof could be adduced demonstrating the regenerating spirit animating the Revelations proclaimed by the Báb and Bahá'u'lláh than their power to transform what can be truly regarded as one of the most backward, the most cowardly, and perverse of peoples into a race of heroes, fit to effect in turn a similar revolution in the life of mankind. To have appeared among a race or nation which by its intrinsic worth and high attainments seemed to warrant the inestimable privilege of being made the receptacle of such a Revelation would in the eyes of an unbelieving world greatly reduce the efficacy of that Message, and detract from the self-sufficiency of its omnipotent power. The contrast so strikingly presented in the pages of Nabíl's Narrative between the heroism that immortalized the life and deeds of the Dawn-Breakers and the degeneracy and cowardice of their defamers and persecutors is in itself a most impressive testimony to the truth of the Message of Him Who had instilled such a spirit into the breasts of His disciples. For any believer of that race to maintain that the excellence of his country and the innate nobility of its people were the fundamental reasons for its being singled out as the primary receptacle of the Revelations of the Báb and Bahá'u'lláh would be untenable in the face of the overwhelming evidence afforded so convincingly by that Narrative.

32   To a lesser degree this principle must of necessity apply to the country which has vindicated its right to be regarded as the cradle of the World Order of Bahá'u'lláh. So great a function, so noble a role, can be regarded as no less inferior to the part played by those immortal souls who, through their sublime renunciation and unparalleled deeds, have been responsible for the birth of the Faith itself. Let not, therefore, those who are to participate so predominantly in the birth of that world civilization, which is the direct offspring of their Faith, imagine for a moment that for some mysterious purpose or by any reason of inherent excellence or special merit Bahá'u'lláh has chosen to confer upon their country and people so great and lasting a distinction. It is precisely by reason of the patent evils which, notwithstanding its other admittedly great characteristics and achievements, an excessive and binding materialism has unfortunately engendered within it that the Author of their Faith and the Center of His Covenant have singled it out to become the standard-bearer of the New World Order envisaged in their writings. It is by such means as this that Bahá'u'lláh can best demon-

strate to a heedless generation His almighty power to raise up from the very midst of a people, immersed in a sea of materialism, a prey to one of the most virulent and long-standing forms of racial prejudice, and notorious for its political corruption, lawlessness and laxity in moral standards, men and women who, as time goes by, will increasingly exemplify those essential virtues of self-renunciation, of moral rectitude, of chastity, of indiscriminating fellowship, of holy discipline, and of spiritual insight that will fit them for the preponderating share they will have in calling into being that World Order and that World Civilization of which their country, no less than the entire human race, stands in desperate need. Theirs will be the duty and privilege, in their capacity first as the establishers of one of the most powerful pillars sustaining the edifice of the Universal House of Justice, and then as the champion-builders of that New World Order of which that House is to be the nucleus and forerunner, to inculcate, demonstrate, and apply those twin and sorely needed principles of Divine justice and order—principles to which the political corruption and the moral license, increasingly staining the society to which they belong, offer so sad and striking a contrast.

Observations such as these, however distasteful and depressing they may be, should not, in the least, blind us to those virtues and qualities of high intelligence, 33 of youthfulness, of unbounded initiative, and enterprise which the nation as a whole so conspicuously displays, and which are being increasingly reflected by the community of the believers within it. Upon these virtues and qualities, no less than upon the elimination of the evils referred to, must depend, to a very great extent, the ability of that community to lay a firm foundation for the country's future role in ushering in the Golden Age of the Cause of Bahá'u'lláh.

34   How great, therefore, how staggering the responsibility that must weigh upon the present generation of the American believers, at this early stage in their spiritual and administrative evolution, to weed out, by every means in their power, those faults, habits, and tendencies which they have inherited from their own nation, and to cultivate, patiently and prayerfully, those distinctive qualities and characteristics that are so indispensable to their effective participation in the great redemptive work of their Faith. Incapable as yet, in view of the restricted size of their community and the limited influence it now wields, of producing any marked effect on the great mass of their countrymen, let them focus their attention, for the present, on their own selves, their own individual needs, their own personal deficiencies and weaknesses, ever mindful that every intensification of effort on their part will better equip them for the time when they will be called upon

to eradicate in their turn such evil tendencies from the lives and the hearts of the entire body of their fellow-citizens. Nor must they overlook the fact that the World Order, whose basis they, as the advance-guard of the future Bahá'í generations of their countrymen, are now laboring to establish, can never be reared unless and until the generality of the people to which they belong has been already purged from the divers ills, whether social or political, that now so severely afflict it.

Surveying as a whole the most pressing needs of this 35 community, attempting to estimate the more serious deficiencies by which it is being handicapped in the discharge of its task, and ever bearing in mind the nature of that still greater task with which it will be forced to wrestle in the future, I feel it my duty to lay special stress upon, and draw the special and urgent attention of the entire body of the American believers, be they young or old, white or colored, teachers or administrators, veterans or newcomers, to what I firmly believe are the essential requirements for the success of the tasks which are now claiming their undivided attention. Great as is the importance of fashioning the outward instruments, and of perfecting the administrative agencies, which they can utilize for the prosecution of their dual task under the Seven Year Plan; vital and urgent as are the campaigns which they are initiating, the schemes and projects which they are devising, and the funds which they are raising, for the efficient conduct of both the Teaching and Temple work, the imponderable, the spiritual, factors, which are bound up with their own individual and inner lives, and with which are associated their human and social relationships, are no less urgent and vital, and demand constant scrutiny, continual self-examination and heart-searching on their part, lest their value be impaired or their vital necessity be obscured or forgotten.

36   Of these spiritual prerequisites of success, which constitute the bedrock on which the security of all teaching plans, Temple projects, and financial schemes, must ultimately rest, the following stand out as preeminent and vital, which the members of the American Bahá'í community will do well to ponder. Upon the extent to which these basic requirements are met, and the manner in which the American believers fulfill them in their individual lives, administrative activities, and social relationships, must depend the measure of the manifold blessings which the All-Bountiful Possessor can vouchsafe to them all. These requirements are none other than a high sense of moral rectitude in their social and administrative activities, absolute chastity in their individual lives, and complete freedom from prejudice in their dealings with peoples of a different race, class, creed, or color.

The first is specially, though not exclusively, directed 37
to their elected representatives, whether local, regional,
or national, who, in their capacity as the custodians
and members of the nascent institutions of the Faith
of Bahá'u'lláh, are shouldering the chief responsibility
in laying an unassailable foundation for that Universal
House of Justice which, as its title implies, is to be the
exponent and guardian of that Divine Justice which
can alone insure the security of, and establish the reign
of law and order in, a strangely disordered world. The
second is mainly and directly concerned with the Bahá'í
youth, who can contribute so decisively to the virility,
the purity, and the driving force of the life of the Bahá'í
community, and upon whom must depend the future
orientation of its destiny, and the complete unfoldment of the potentialities with which God has endowed
it. The third should be the immediate, the universal,
and the chief concern of all and sundry members of
the Bahá'í community, of whatever age, rank, experience, class, or color, as all, with no exception, must
face its challenging implications, and none can claim,
however much he may have progressed along this line,
to have completely discharged the stern responsibilities which it inculcates.

A rectitude of conduct, an abiding sense of undevi- 38
ating justice, unobscured by the demoralizing influences

which a corruption-ridden political life so strikingly manifests; a chaste, pure, and holy life, unsullied and unclouded by the indecencies, the vices, the false standards, which an inherently deficient moral code tolerates, perpetuates, and fosters; a fraternity freed from that cancerous growth of racial prejudice, which is eating into the vitals of an already debilitated society—these are the ideals which the American believers must, from now on, individually and through concerted action, strive to promote, in both their private and public lives, ideals which are the chief propelling forces that can most effectively accelerate the march of their institutions, plans, and enterprises, that can guard the honor and integrity of their Faith, and subdue any obstacles that may confront it in the future.

39   This rectitude of conduct, with its implications of justice, equity, truthfulness, honesty, fair-mindedness, reliability, and trustworthiness, must distinguish every phase of the life of the Bahá'í community. *"The companions of God,"* Bahá'u'lláh Himself has declared, *"are, in this day, the lump that must leaven the peoples of the world. They must show forth such trustworthiness, such truthfulness and perseverance, such deeds and character that all mankind may profit by their example." "I swear by Him Who is the Most Great Ocean!"* He again affirms, *"Within the very breath of such souls as are pure and sanctified far-reaching potentialities are hidden. So great*

are these potentialities that they exercise their influence upon all created things." "He is the true servant of God," He, in another passage has written, "who, in this day, were he to pass through cities of silver and gold, would not deign to look upon them, and whose heart would remain pure and undefiled from whatever things can be seen in this world, be they its goods or its treasures. I swear by the Sun of Truth! The breath of such a man is endowed with potency, and his words with attraction." "By Him Who shineth above the Daypring of sanctity!" He, still more emphatically, has revealed, "If the whole earth were to be converted into silver and gold, no man who can be said to have truly ascended into the heaven of faith and certitude would deign to regard it, much less to seize and keep it. . . . They who dwell within the Tabernacle of God, and are established upon the seats of everlasting glory, will refuse, though they be dying of hunger, to stretch their hands, and seize unlawfully the property of their neighbor, however vile and worthless he may be. The purpose of the one true God in manifesting Himself is to summon all mankind to truthfulness and sincerity, to piety and trustworthiness, to resignation and submissiveness to the will of God, to forbearance and kindliness, to uprightness and wisdom. His object is to array every man with the mantle of a saintly character, and to adorn him with the ornament of holy and goodly deeds." "We have admonished all the loved ones of God," He insists, "to take heed lest the hem of Our sacred vesture be smirched with the mire of unlawful deeds, or be stained with the dust of reprehensible conduct." "Cleave unto righteousness, O people of Bahá," He thus exhorts them, "This, verily, is the commandment which this wronged One hath given unto you, and the first choice of His unrestrained will for every one of you." "A good character," He explains, "is, verily, the best mantle for men from God. With it He adorneth the temples of His loved ones. By My life! The light of a good character surpasseth the light of the sun and the radiance thereof." "One righteous act," He, again, has written, "is endowed with a potency that can so elevate the dust as to cause it to pass beyond the heaven of heavens. It can tear every bond asunder, and hath the power to restore the force that hath spent itself and vanished. . . . Be pure, O people of God, be pure; be righteous, be righteous. . . . Say: O people of God! That which can insure the victory of Him Who is the Eternal Truth, His hosts and helpers on earth, have been set down in the sacred Books and Scriptures, and are as clear and manifest as the sun. These hosts are such righteous deeds, such conduct and character, as are acceptable in His sight. Whoso ariseth, in this Day, to aid Our Cause, and summoneth to his assistance the hosts of a praiseworthy character and upright conduct, the influence from such an action will, most certainly, be diffused throughout the whole world." "The betterment of the world," is yet another statement, "can be accomplished *through pure and goodly deeds, through commendable and seemly conduct."* "Be fair to yourselves and to others," He thus counseleth them, *"that the evidences of justice may be revealed through your deeds among Our faithful servants."* "Equity," He also has written, *"is the most fundamental among human virtues. The evaluation of all things must needs depend upon it."* And again, *"Observe equity in your judgment, ye men of understanding heart! He that is unjust in his judgment is destitute of the characteristics that distinguish man's station."* "Beautify your tongues, O people," He further admonishes them, *"with truthfulness, and adorn your souls with the ornament of honesty. Beware, O people, that ye deal not treacherously with anyone. Be ye the trustees of God amongst His creatures, and the emblems of His generosity amidst His people."* "Let your eye be chaste," is yet another counsel, *"your hand faithful, your tongue truthful, and your heart enlightened."* "Be an ornament to the countenance of truth," is yet another admonition, *"a crown to the brow of fidelity, a pillar of the temple of righteousness, a breath of life to the body of mankind, an ensign of the hosts of justice, a luminary above the horizon of virtue."* "Let truthfulness and courtesy be your adorning," is still another admonition; *"suffer not yourselves to be deprived of the robe of forbearance and justice, that the sweet savors of holiness may be wafted from your hearts upon all created things. Say: Beware, O people of Bahá, lest ye walk in the ways of them whose words differ from their deeds. Strive that ye may be enabled to manifest to the peoples of the earth the signs of God, and to mirror forth His command- ments. Let your acts be a guide unto all mankind, for the professions of most men, be they high or low, differ from their conduct. It is through your deeds that ye can distin- guish yourselves from others. Through them the brightness of your light can be shed upon the whole earth. Happy is the man that heedeth My counsel, and keepeth the precepts prescribed by Him Who is the All-Knowing, the All-Wise.*"

40   "*O army of God!* " writes 'Abdu'l-Bahá, "*Through the protection and help vouchsafed by the Blessed Beauty— may my life be a sacrifice to His loved ones—ye must con- duct yourselves in such a manner that ye may stand out distinguished and brilliant as the sun among other souls. Should any one of you enter a city, he should become a center of attraction by reason of his sincerity, his faithful- ness and love, his honesty and fidelity, his truthfulness and loving-kindness towards all the peoples of the world, so that the people of that city may cry out and say: 'This man is unquestionably a Bahá'í, for his manners, his be- havior, his conduct, his morals, his nature, and disposi- tion reflect the attributes of the Bahá'ís.' Not until ye at- tain this station can ye be said to have been faithful to the Covenant and Testament of God.*" "*The most vital duty, in this day,*" He, moreover, has written, "*is to purify*

your characters, to correct your manners, and improve your conduct. The beloved of the Merciful must show forth such character and conduct among His creatures, that the fragrance of their holiness may be shed upon the whole world, and may quicken the dead, inasmuch as the purpose of the Manifestation of God and the dawning of the limitless lights of the Invisible is to educate the souls of men, and refine the character of every living man. . . ." "Truthfulness," He asserts, *"is the foundation of all human virtues. Without truthfulness progress and success, in all the worlds of God, are impossible for any soul. When this holy attribute is established in man, all the divine qualities will also be acquired."*

Such a rectitude of conduct must manifest itself, 41 with ever-increasing potency, in every verdict which the elected representatives of the Bahá'í community, in whatever capacity they may find themselves, may be called upon to pronounce. It must be constantly reflected in the business dealings of all its members, in their domestic lives, in all manner of employment, and in any service they may, in the future, render their government or people. It must be exemplified in the conduct of all Bahá'í electors, when exercising their sacred rights and functions. It must characterize the attitude of every loyal believer towards nonacceptance of political posts, nonidentification with political parties, nonparticipation in political controversies, and nonmembership in political organizations and ecclesiastical institutions. It must reveal itself in the uncompromising adherence of all, whether young or old, to the clearly enunciated and fundamental principles laid down by 'Abdu'l-Bahá in His addresses, and to the laws and ordinances revealed by Bahá'u'lláh in His Most Holy Book. It must be demonstrated in the impartiality of every defender of the Faith against its enemies, in his fair-mindedness in recognizing any merits that enemy may possess, and in his honesty in discharging any obligations he may have towards him. It must constitute the brightest ornament of the life, the pursuits, the exertions, and the utterances of every Bahá'í teacher, whether laboring at home or abroad, whether in the front ranks of the teaching force, or occupying a less active and responsible position. It must be made the hallmark of that numerically small, yet intensely dynamic and highly responsible body of the elected national representatives of every Bahá'í community, which constitutes the sustaining pillar, and the sole instrument for the election, in every community, of that Universal House whose very name and title, as ordained by Bahá'u'lláh, symbolizes that rectitude of conduct which is its highest mission to safeguard and enforce.

42 So great and transcendental is this principle of Divine justice, a principle that must be regarded as the crowning distinction of all Local and National Assem-

blies, in their capacity as forerunners of the Universal House of Justice, that Bahá'u'lláh Himself subordinates His personal inclination and wish to the all-compelling force of its demands and implications. *"God is My witness!"* He thus explains, *"were it not contrary to the Law of God, I would have kissed the hand of My would-be murderer, and would cause him to inherit My earthly goods. I am restrained, however, by the binding Law laid down in the Book, and am Myself bereft of all worldly possessions."* *"Know thou, of a truth,"* He significantly affirms, *"these great oppressions that have befallen the world are preparing it for the advent of the Most Great Justice."* *"Say,"* He again asserts, *"He hath appeared with that Justice wherewith mankind hath been adorned, and yet the people are, for the most part, asleep."* *"The light of men is Justice,"* He moreover states, *"Quench it not with the contrary winds of oppression and tyranny. The purpose of justice is the appearance of unity among men."* *"No radiance,"* He declares, *"can compare with that of justice. The organization of the world and the tranquillity of mankind depend upon it."* *"O people of God!"* He exclaims, *"That which traineth the world is Justice, for it is upheld by two pillars, reward and punishment. These two pillars are the sources of life to the world."* *"Justice and equity,"* is yet another assertion, *"are two guardians for the protection of man. They have appeared arrayed in their mighty and sacred names to maintain the world in* uprightness and protect the nations." "Bestir yourselves, O people," is His emphatic warning, "in anticipation of the days of Divine justice, for the promised hour is now come. Beware lest ye fail to apprehend its import, and be accounted among the erring." "The day is approaching," He similarly has written, "when the faithful will behold the daystar of justice shining in its full splendor from the dayspring of glory." "The shame I was made to bear," He significantly remarks, "hath uncovered the glory with which the whole of creation had been invested, and through the cruelties I have endured, the daystar of justice hath manifested itself, and shed its splendor upon men." "The world," He again has written, "is in great turmoil, and the minds of its people are in a state of utter confusion. We entreat the Almighty that He may graciously illuminate them with the glory of His Justice, and enable them to discover that which will be profitable unto them at all times and under all conditions." And again, "There can be no doubt whatever that if the daystar of justice, which the clouds of tyranny have obscured, were to shed its light upon men, the face of the earth would be completely transformed."

43   "God be praised!" 'Abdu'l-Bahá, in His turn, exclaims, "The sun of justice hath risen above the horizon of Bahá'u'lláh. For in His Tablets the foundations of such a justice have been laid as no mind hath, from the beginning of creation, conceived." "The canopy of existence,"

He further explains, *"resteth upon the pole of justice, and not of forgiveness, and the life of mankind dependeth on justice and not on forgiveness."*

44 Small wonder, therefore, that the Author of the Bahá'í Revelation should have chosen to associate the name and title of that House, which is to be the crowning glory of His administrative institutions, not with forgiveness but with justice, to have made justice the only basis and the permanent foundation of His Most Great Peace, and to have proclaimed it in His Hidden Words as *"the best beloved of all things"* in His sight. It is to the American believers, particularly, that I feel urged to direct this fervent plea to ponder in their hearts the implications of this moral rectitude, and to uphold, with heart and soul and uncompromisingly, both individually and collectively, this sublime standard— a standard of which justice is so essential and potent an element.

45 As to a chaste and holy life, it should be regarded as no less essential a factor that must contribute its proper share to the strengthening and vitalization of the Bahá'í community, upon which must in turn depend the success of any Bahá'í plan or enterprise. In these days when the forces of irreligion are weakening the moral fiber, and undermining the foundations of individual morality, the obligation of chastity and holiness must claim an increasing share of the attention of the American

believers, both in their individual capacities and as the responsible custodians of the interests of the Faith of Bahá'u'lláh. In the discharge of such an obligation, to which the special circumstances resulting from an excessive and enervating materialism now prevailing in their country lend particular significance, they must play a conspicuous and predominant role. All of them, be they men or women, must, at this threatening hour when the lights of religion are fading out, and its restraints are one by one being abolished, pause to examine themselves, scrutinize their conduct, and with characteristic resolution arise to purge the life of their community of every trace of moral laxity that might stain the name, or impair the integrity, of so holy and precious a Faith.

46   A chaste and holy life must be made the controlling principle in the behavior and conduct of all Bahá'ís, both in their social relations with the members of their own community, and in their contact with the world at large. It must adorn and reinforce the ceaseless labors and meritorious exertions of those whose enviable position is to propagate the Message, and to administer the affairs, of the Faith of Bahá'u'lláh. It must be upheld, in all its integrity and implications, in every phase of the life of those who fill the ranks of that Faith, whether in their homes, their travels, their clubs, their societies, their entertainments, their schools,

and their universities. It must be accorded special consideration in the conduct of the social activities of every Bahá'í summer school and any other occasions on which Bahá'í community life is organized and fostered. It must be closely and continually identified with the mission of the Bahá'í youth, both as an element in the life of the Bahá'í community, and as a factor in the future progress and orientation of the youth of their own country.

Such a chaste and holy life, with its implications of 47 modesty, purity, temperance, decency, and clean-mindedness, involves no less than the exercise of moderation in all that pertains to dress, language, amusements, and all artistic and literary avocations. It demands daily vigilance in the control of one's carnal desires and corrupt inclinations. It calls for the abandonment of a frivolous conduct, with its excessive attachment to trivial and often misdirected pleasures. It requires total abstinence from all alcoholic drinks, from opium, and from similar habit-forming drugs. It condemns the prostitution of art and of literature, the practices of nudism and of companionate marriage, infidelity in marital relationships, and all manner of promiscuity, of easy familiarity, and of sexual vices. It can tolerate no compromise with the theories, the standards, the habits, and the excesses of a decadent age. Nay rather it seeks to demonstrate, through the dynamic force of its example, the pernicious character of such theories, the falsity of such standards, the hollowness of such claims, the perversity of such habits, and the sacrilegious character of such excesses.

48 *"By the righteousness of God!"* writes Bahá'u'lláh, *"The world, its vanities and its glory, and whatever delights it can offer, are all, in the sight of God, as worthless as, nay even more contemptible than, dust and ashes. Would that the hearts of men could comprehend it. Wash yourselves thoroughly, O people of Bahá, from the defilement of the world, and of all that pertaineth unto it. God Himself beareth Me witness! The things of the earth ill beseem you. Cast them away unto such as may desire them, and fasten your eyes upon this most holy and effulgent Vision."* *"O ye My loved ones!"* He thus exhorts His followers, *"Suffer not the hem of My sacred vesture to be smirched and mired with the things of this world, and follow not the promptings of your evil and corrupt desires."* And again, *"O ye the beloved of the one true God! Pass beyond the narrow retreats of your evil and corrupt desires, and advance into the vast immensity of the realm of God, and abide ye in the meads of sanctity and of detachment, that the fragrance of your deeds may lead the whole of mankind to the ocean of God's unfading glory."* *"Disencumber yourselves,"* He thus commands them, *"of all attachment to this world and the vanities thereof. Beware that ye approach them not, inasmuch as they prompt you to walk*

after your own lusts and covetous desires, and hinder you from entering the straight and glorious Path." "*Eschew all manner of wickedness,*" is His commandment, "*for such things are forbidden unto you in the Book which none touch except such as God hath cleansed from every taint of guilt, and numbered among the purified.*" "*A race of men,*" is His written promise, "*incomparable in charac-ter, shall be raised up which, with the feet of detachment, will tread under all who are in heaven and on earth, and will cast the sleeve of holiness over all that hath been cre-ated from water and clay.*" "*The civilization,*" is His grave warning, "*so often vaunted by the learned exponents of arts and sciences, will, if allowed to overleap the bounds of moderation, bring great evil upon men. . . . If carried to excess, civilization will prove as prolific a source of evil as it had been of goodness when kept within the restraints of moderation.*" "*He hath chosen out of the whole world the hearts of His servants,*" He explains, "*and made them each a seat for the revelation of His glory. Wherefore, sanc-tify them from every defilement, that the things for which they were created may be engraven upon them. This in-deed is a token of God's bountiful favor.*" "*Say,*" He pro-claims, "*He is not to be numbered with the people of Bahá who followeth his mundane desires, or fixeth his heart on things of the earth. He is My true follower who, if he come to a valley of pure gold will pass straight through it aloof as a cloud, and will neither turn back, nor pause.*

Such a man is assuredly of Me. From his garment the Concourse on high can inhale the fragrance of sanctity. . . . And if he met the fairest and most comely of women, he would not feel his heart seduced by the least shadow of desire for her beauty. Such an one indeed is the creation of spotless chastity. Thus instructeth you the Pen of the Ancient of Days, as bidden by your Lord, the Almighty, the All-Bountiful." "*They that follow their lusts and corrupt inclinations,*"is yet another warning, "*have erred and dissipated their efforts. They indeed are of the lost." "It behooveth the people of Bahá,"* He also has written, "*to die to the world and all that is therein, to be so detached from all earthly things that the inmates of Paradise may inhale from their garment the sweet smelling savor of sanctity. . . . They that have tarnished the fair name of the Cause of God by following the things of the flesh—these are in palpable error!" "Purity and chastity,"* He particularly admonishes, "*have been, and still are, the most great ornaments for the handmaidens of God. God is My Witness! The brightness of the light of chastity sheddeth its illumination upon the worlds of the spirit, and its fragrance is wafted even unto the Most Exalted Paradise."* "*God,"* He again affirms, "*hath verily made chastity to be a crown for the heads of His handmaidens. Great is the blessedness of that handmaiden that hath attained unto this great station." "We, verily, have decreed in Our Book,"* is His assurance, "*a goodly and bountiful reward to who-*

soever will turn away from wickedness, and lead a chaste and godly life. He, in truth, is the Great Giver, the All-Bountiful." "We have sustained the weight of all calamities," He testifies, *"to sanctify you from all earthly corruption and ye are yet indifferent. . . . We, verily, behold your actions. If We perceive from them the sweet smelling savor of purity and holiness, We will most certainly bless you. Then will the tongues of the inmates of Paradise utter your praise and magnify your names amidst them who have drawn nigh unto God."*

"The drinking of wine," writes 'Abdu'l-Bahá, *"is, according to the text of the Most Holy Book, forbidden; for it is the cause of chronic diseases, weakeneth the nerves, and consumeth the mind." "Drink ye, O handmaidens of God,"* Bahá'u'lláh Himself has affirmed, *"the Mystic Wine from the cup of My words. Cast away, then, from you that which your minds abhor, for it hath been forbidden unto you in His Tablets and His Scriptures. Beware lest ye barter away the River that is life indeed for that which the souls of the pure-hearted detest. Become ye intoxicated with the wine of the love of God, and not with that which deadeneth your minds, O ye that adore Him! Verily, it hath been forbidden unto every believer, whether man or woman. Thus hath the sun of My commandment shone forth above the horizon of My utterance, that the handmaidens who believe in Me may be illumined."* 49

50   It must be remembered, however, that the maintenance of such a high standard of moral conduct is not to be associated or confused with any form of asceticism, or of excessive and bigoted puritanism. The standard inculcated by Bahá'u'lláh seeks, under no circumstances, to deny anyone the legitimate right and privilege to derive the fullest advantage and benefit from the manifold joys, beauties, and pleasures with which the world has been so plentifully enriched by an All-Loving Creator. *"Should a man,"* Bahá'u'lláh Himself reassures us, *"wish to adorn himself with the ornaments of the earth, to wear its apparels, or partake of the benefits it can bestow, no harm can befall him, if he alloweth nothing whatever to intervene between him and God, for God hath ordained every good thing, whether created in the heavens or in the earth, for such of His servants as truly believe in Him. Eat ye, O people, of the good things which God hath allowed you, and deprive not yourselves from His wondrous bounties. Render thanks and praise unto Him, and be of them that are truly thankful."*

51   As to racial prejudice, the corrosion of which, for well-nigh a century, has bitten into the fiber, and attacked the whole social structure of American society, it should be regarded as constituting the most vital and challenging issue confronting the Bahá'í community at the present stage of its evolution. The ceaseless exertions which this issue of paramount impor-

tance calls for, the sacrifices it must impose, the care and vigilance it demands, the moral courage and fortitude it requires, the tact and sympathy it necessitates, invest this problem, which the American believers are still far from having satisfactorily resolved, with an urgency and importance that cannot be overestimated. White and Negro, high and low, young and old, whether newly converted to the Faith or not, all who stand identified with it must participate in, and lend their assistance, each according to his or her capacity, experience, and opportunities, to the common task of fulfilling the instructions, realizing the hopes, and following the example, of 'Abdu'l-Bahá. Whether colored or noncolored, neither race has the right, or can conscientiously claim, to be regarded as absolved from such an obligation, as having realized such hopes, or having faithfully followed such an example. A long and thorny road, beset with pitfalls, still remains untraveled, both by the white and the Negro exponents of the redeeming Faith of Bahá'u'lláh. On the distance they cover, and the manner in which they travel that road, must depend, to an extent which few among them can imagine, the operation of those intangible influences which are indispensable to the spiritual triumph of the American believers and the material success of their newly launched enterprise.

52 Let them call to mind, fearlessly and determinedly, the example and conduct of 'Abdu'l-Bahá while in their midst. Let them remember His courage, His genuine love, His informal and indiscriminating fellowship, His contempt for and impatience of criticism, tempered by His tact and wisdom. Let them revive and perpetuate the memory of those unforgettable and historic episodes and occasions on which He so strikingly demonstrated His keen sense of justice, His spontaneous sympathy for the downtrodden, His ever-abiding sense of the oneness of the human race, His overflowing love for its members, and His displeasure with those who dared to flout His wishes, to deride His methods, to challenge His principles, or to nullify His acts.

53 To discriminate against any race, on the ground of its being socially backward, politically immature, and numerically in a minority, is a flagrant violation of the spirit that animates the Faith of Bahá'u'lláh. The consciousness of any division or cleavage in its ranks is alien to its very purpose, principles, and ideals. Once its members have fully recognized the claim of its Author, and, by identifying themselves with its Administrative Order, accepted unreservedly the principles and laws embodied in its teachings, every differentiation of class, creed, or color must automatically be obliterated, and never be allowed, under any pretext, and however great the pressure of events or of public opinion, to

reassert itself. If any discrimination is at all to be tolerated, it should be a discrimination not against, but rather in favor of the minority, be it racial or otherwise. Unlike the nations and peoples of the earth, be they of the East or of the West, democratic or authoritarian, communist or capitalist, whether belonging to the Old World or the New, who either ignore, trample upon, or extirpate, the racial, religious, or political minorities within the sphere of their jurisdiction, every organized community enlisted under the banner of Bahá'u'lláh should feel it to be its first and inescapable obligation to nurture, encourage, and safeguard every minority belonging to any faith, race, class, or nation within it. So great and vital is this principle that in such circumstances, as when an equal number of ballots have been cast in an election, or where the qualifications for any office are balanced as between the various races, faiths or nationalities within the community, priority should unhesitatingly be accorded the party representing the minority, and this for no other reason except to stimulate and encourage it, and afford it an opportunity to further the interests of the community. In the light of this principle, and bearing in mind the extreme desirability of having the minority elements participate and share responsibility in the conduct of Bahá'í activity, it should be the duty of every Bahá'í community so to arrange its affairs that in cases where individuals belonging to the divers minority elements within it are already qualified and fulfill the necessary requirements, Bahá'í representative institutions, be they Assemblies, conventions, conferences, or committees, may have represented on them as many of these divers elements, racial or otherwise, as possible. The adoption of such a course, and faithful adherence to it, would not only be a source of inspiration and encouragement to those elements that are numerically small and inadequately represented, but would demonstrate to the world at large the universality and representative character of the Faith of Bahá'u'lláh, and the freedom of His followers from the taint of those prejudices which have already wrought such havoc in the domestic affairs, as well as the foreign relationships, of the nations.

54   Freedom from racial prejudice, in any of its forms, should, at such a time as this when an increasingly large section of the human race is falling a victim to its devastating ferocity, be adopted as the watchword of the entire body of the American believers, in whichever state they reside, in whatever circles they move, whatever their age, traditions, tastes, and habits. It should be consistently demonstrated in every phase of their activity and life, whether in the Bahá'í community or outside it, in public or in private, formally as well as informally, individually as well as in their official ca-

pacity as organized groups, committees and Assemblies. It should be deliberately cultivated through the various and everyday opportunities, no matter how insignificant, that present themselves, whether in their homes, their business offices, their schools and colleges, their social parties and recreation grounds, their Bahá'í meetings, conferences, conventions, summer schools and Assemblies. It should, above all else, become the keynote of the policy of that august body which, in its capacity as the national representative, and the director and coordinator of the affairs of the community, must set the example, and facilitate the application of such a vital principle to the lives and activities of those whose interests it safeguards and represents.

"O ye discerning ones!" Bahá'u'lláh has written, *"Verily, the words which have descended from the heaven of the Will of God are the source of unity and harmony for the world. Close your eyes to racial differences, and welcome all with the light of oneness." "We desire but the good of the world and the happiness of the nations,"* He proclaims, *". . . that all nations should become one in faith and all men as brothers; that the bonds of affection and unity between the sons of men should be strengthened; that diversity of religion should cease, and differences of race be annulled." "Bahá'u'lláh hath said,"* writes 'Abdu'l-Bahá, *"that the various races of humankind lend a composite harmony and beauty of color to the whole.* 55

Let all associate, therefore, in this great human garden even as flowers grow and blend together side by side without discord or disagreement between them." "Bahá'u'lláh," 'Abdu'l-Bahá moreover has said, *"once compared the colored people to the black pupil of the eye surrounded by the white. In this black pupil is seen the reflection of that which is before it, and through it the light of the spirit shineth forth."*

56   *"God,"* 'Abdu'l-Bahá Himself declares, *"maketh no distinction between the white and the black. If the hearts are pure both are acceptable unto Him. God is no respecter of persons on account of either color or race. All colors are acceptable unto Him, be they white, black, or yellow. Inasmuch as all were created in the image of God, we must bring ourselves to realize that all embody divine possibilities." "In the estimation of God,"* He states, *"all men are equal. There is no distinction or preference for any soul, in the realm of His justice and equity." "God did not make these divisions,"* He affirms; *"these divisions have had their origin in man himself. Therefore, as they are against the plan and purpose of God they are false and imaginary." "In the estimation of God,"* He again affirms, *"there is no distinction of color; all are one in the color and beauty of servitude to Him. Color is not important; the heart is all-important. It mattereth not what the exterior may be if the heart is pure and white within. God doth not behold differences of hue and complexion. He looketh at the hearts.*

He whose morals and virtues are praiseworthy is preferred in the presence of God; he who is devoted to the Kingdom is most beloved. In the realm of genesis and creation the question of color is of least importance." "Throughout the animal kingdom," He explains, *"we do not find the creatures separated because of color. They recognize unity of species and oneness of kind. If we do not find color distinction drawn in a kingdom of lower intelligence and reason, how can it be justified among human beings, especially when we know that all have come from the same source and belong to the same household? In origin and intention of creation mankind is one. Distinctions of race and color have arisen afterward." "Man is endowed with superior reasoning power and the faculty of perception";* He further explains, *"he is the manifestation of divine bestowals. Shall racial ideas prevail and obscure the creative purpose of unity in his kingdom?" "One of the important questions,"* He significantly remarks, *"which affect the unity and the solidarity of mankind is the fellowship and equality of the white and colored races. Between these two races certain points of agreement and points of distinction exist which warrant just and mutual consideration. The points of contact are many. . . . In this country, the United States of America, patriotism is common to both races; all have equal rights to citizenship, speak one language, receive the blessings of the same civilization, and follow the precepts of the same religion. In fact*

*numerous points of partnership and agreement exist be-
tween the two races, whereas the one point of distinction
is that of color. Shall this, the least of all distinctions, be
allowed to separate you as races and individuals?"* "This
variety in forms and coloring,"*He stresses,* "which is manifest in all the kingdoms is according to creative Wisdom
and hath a divine purpose."* "The diversity in the human
family,"* He claims,* "should be the cause of love and harmony, as it is in music where many different notes blend
together in the making of a perfect chord."* "If you meet,"*
is His admonition,* "those of a different race and color
from yourself, do not mistrust them, and withdraw yourself into your shell of conventionality, but rather be glad
and show them kindness."* "In the world of being,"* He
testifies,* "the meeting is blessed when the white and colored races meet together with infinite spiritual love and
heavenly harmony. When such meetings are established,
and the participants associate with each other with perfect
love, unity and kindness, the angels of the Kingdom praise
them, and the Beauty of Bahá'u'lláh addresseth them,
'Blessed are ye! Blessed are ye!'"* "When a gathering of
these two races is brought about,"* He likewise asserts,*
"that assemblage will become the magnet of the Concourse
on high, and the confirmation of the Blessed Beauty will
surround it."* "Strive earnestly,"* He again exhorts both
races,* "and put forth your greatest endeavor toward the
accomplishment of this fellowship and the cementing of*

this bond of brotherhood between you. Such an attainment is not possible without will and effort on the part of each; from one, expressions of gratitude and appreciation; from the other, kindliness and recognition of equality. Each one should endeavor to develop and assist the other toward mutual advancement. . . . Love and unity will be fostered between you, thereby bringing about the oneness of mankind. For the accomplishment of unity between the colored and white will be an assurance of the world's peace." "I hope," He thus addresses members of the white race, *"that ye may cause that downtrodden race to become glorious, and to be joined with the white race, to serve the world of man with the utmost sincerity, faithfulness, love, and purity. This opposition, enmity, and prejudice among the white race and the colored cannot be effaced except through faith, assurance, and the teachings of the Blessed Beauty."* "This question of the union of the white and the black is very important," He warns, *"for if it is not realized, erelong great difficulties will arise, and harmful results will follow."* "If this matter remaineth without change," is yet another warning, *"enmity will be increased day by day, and the final result will be hardship and may end in bloodshed."*

A tremendous effort is required by both races if their outlook, their manners, and conduct are to reflect, in this darkened age, the spirit and teachings of the Faith of Bahá'u'lláh. Casting away once and for all the falla-

57

cious doctrine of racial superiority, with all its attendant evils, confusion, and miseries, and welcoming and encouraging the intermixture of races, and tearing down the barriers that now divide them, they should each endeavor, day and night, to fulfill their particular responsibilities in the common task which so urgently faces them. Let them, while each is attempting to contribute its share to the solution of this perplexing problem, call to mind the warnings of 'Abdu'l-Bahá, and visualize, while there is yet time, the dire consequences that must follow if this challenging and unhappy situation that faces the entire American nation is not definitely remedied.

58 Let the white make a supreme effort in their resolve to contribute their share to the solution of this problem, to abandon once for all their usually inherent and at times subconscious sense of superiority, to correct their tendency towards revealing a patronizing attitude towards the members of the other race, to persuade them through their intimate, spontaneous and informal association with them of the genuineness of their friendship and the sincerity of their intentions, and to master their impatience of any lack of responsiveness on the part of a people who have received, for so long a period, such grievous and slow-healing wounds. Let the Negroes, through a corresponding effort on their part, show by every means in their power the warmth

of their response, their readiness to forget the past, and their ability to wipe out every trace of suspicion that may still linger in their hearts and minds. Let neither think that the solution of so vast a problem is a matter that exclusively concerns the other. Let neither think that such a problem can either easily or immediately be resolved. Let neither think that they can wait confidently for the solution of this problem until the initiative has been taken, and the favorable circumstances created, by agencies that stand outside the orbit of their Faith. Let neither think that anything short of genuine love, extreme patience, true humility, consummate tact, sound initiative, mature wisdom, and deliberate, persistent, and prayerful effort, can succeed in blotting out the stain which this patent evil has left on the fair name of their common country. Let them rather believe, and be firmly convinced, that on their mutual understanding, their amity, and sustained cooperation, must depend, more than on any other force or organization operating outside the circle of their Faith, the deflection of that dangerous course so greatly feared by 'Abdu'l-Bahá, and the materialization of the hopes He cherished for their joint contribution to the fulfillment of that country's glorious destiny.

Dearly beloved friends! A rectitude of conduct 59 which, in all its manifestations, offers a striking contrast to the deceitfulness and corruption that charac-

Weapons to:
Regeneration within the Bahai community:
holiness, interracial friendships.
Chastity, Rectitude of Conduct, no moral laxity

terize the political life of the nation and of the parties
and factions that compose it; a holiness and chastity
that are diametrically opposed to the moral laxity and
licentiousness which defile the character of a not inconsiderable proportion of its citizens; an interracial
fellowship completely purged from the curse of racial
prejudice which stigmatizes the vast majority of its
people—these are the weapons which the American
believers can and must wield in their double crusade,
first to regenerate the inward life of their own community, and next to assail the long-standing evils that have
entrenched themselves in the life of their nation. The
perfection of such weapons, the wise and effective uti-
lization of every one of them, more than the furtherance of any particular plan, or the devising of any special scheme, or the accumulation of any amount of
material resources, can prepare them for the time when
the Hand of Destiny will have directed them to assist
in creating and in bringing into operation that World
Order which is now incubating within the worldwide
administrative institutions of their Faith.

60   In the conduct of this twofold crusade the valiant
warriors struggling in the name and for the Cause of
Bahá'u'lláh must, of necessity, encounter stiff resistance,
and suffer many a setback. Their own instincts, no less
than the fury of conservative forces, the opposition of
vested interests, and the objections of a corrupt and

pleasure-seeking generation, must be reckoned with, resolutely resisted, and completely overcome. As their defensive measures for the impending struggle are organized and extended, storms of abuse and ridicule, and campaigns of condemnation and misrepresentation, may be unloosed against them. Their Faith, they may soon find, has been assaulted, their motives misconstrued, their aims defamed, their aspirations derided, their institutions scorned, their influence belittled, their authority undermined, and their Cause, at times, deserted by a few who will either be incapable of appreciating the nature of their ideals, or unwilling to bear the brunt of the mounting criticisms which such a contest is sure to involve. *"Because of 'Abdu'l-Bahá,"* the beloved Master has prophesied, *"many a test will be visited upon you. Troubles will befall you, and suffering afflict you."*

Let not, however, the invincible army of Bahá'u'lláh, 61 who in the West, and at one of its potential storm centers is to fight, in His name and for His sake, one of its fiercest and most glorious battles, be afraid of any criticism that might be directed against it. Let it not be deterred by any condemnation with which the tongue of the slanderer may seek to debase its motives. Let it not recoil before the threatening advance of the forces of fanaticism, of orthodoxy, of corruption, and of prejudice that may be leagued against it. The voice of criticism is a voice that indirectly reinforces the proclamation of its Cause. Unpopularity but serves to throw into greater relief the contrast between it and its adversaries, while ostracism is itself the magnetic power that must eventually win over to its camp the most vociferous and inveterate amongst its foes. Already in the land where the greatest battles of the Faith have been fought, and its most rapacious enemies have lived, the march of events, the slow yet steady infiltration of its ideals, and the fulfillment of its prophecies, have resulted not only in disarming and in transforming the character of some of its most redoubtable enemies, but also in securing their firm and unreserved allegiance to its Founders. So complete a transformation, so startling a reversal of attitude, can only be effected if that chosen vehicle which is designed to carry the Message of Bahá'-u'lláh to the hungry, the restless, and unshepherded multitudes is itself thoroughly cleansed from the defilements which it seeks to remove.

62 It is upon you, therefore, my best-beloved friends, that I wish to impress not only the urgency and imperative necessity of your holy task, but also the limitless possibilities which it possesses of raising to such an exalted level not only the life and activities of your own community, but the motives and standards that govern the relationships existing among the people to which you belong. Undismayed by the formidable nature of

this task, you will, I am confident, meet as befits you the challenge of these times, so fraught with peril, so full of corruption, and yet so pregnant with the promise of a future so bright that no previous age in the annals of mankind can rival its glory.

Dearly beloved friends! I have attempted, in the beginning of these pages, to convey an idea of the glorious opportunities as well as the tremendous responsibilities which, as a result of the persecution of the far-flung Faith of Bahá'u'lláh, now face the community of the American believers, at so critical a stage in the Formative Period of their Faith, and in so crucial an epoch in the world's history. I have dwelt sufficiently upon the character of the mission which in a not too distant future that community must, through the impelling force of circumstances, arise and carry out. I have uttered the warning which I felt would be necessary to a clearer understanding, and a better discharge, of the tasks lying ahead of it. I have set forth, and stressed as far as it was in my power, those exalted and dynamic virtues, those lofty standards, which, difficult as they are to attain, constitute nonetheless the essential requirements for the success of those tasks. A word, I believe, should now be said in connection with the material aspect of their immediate task, upon the termination of which, at its appointed time, must de-

63

pend not only the unfoldment of the subsequent stages in the Divine Plan envisaged by 'Abdu'l-Bahá, but also the acquisition of those capacities which will qualify them to discharge, in the fullness of time, the duties and responsibilities demanded by that greater mission which it is their privilege to perform.

64   The Seven Year Plan, with its twofold aspects of Temple ornamentation and extension of teaching activity, embracing both the Northern and Southern American continents, is now well advanced into its second year, and offers to anyone who has observed its progress in recent months signs that are extremely heartening and which augur well for the attainment of its objectives within the allotted time. The successive steps designed to facilitate, and covering the entire field of, the work to be achieved in connection with the exterior ornamentation of the Temple have for the most part been taken. The final phase which is to mark the triumphant conclusion of a thirty-year old enterprise has at long last been entered. The initial contract connected with the first and main story of that historic edifice has been signed. The Fund associated with the beloved name of the Greatest Holy Leaf has been launched. The uninterrupted continuation to its very end of so laudable an enterprise is now assured. The poignant memories of one whose heart so greatly rejoiced at the rearing of the superstructure of this sa-

cred House will so energize the final exertions required to complete it as to dissipate any doubt that may yet linger in any mind as to the capacity of its builders to worthily consummate their task.

The teaching aspect of the Plan must now be pondered. Its challenge must be met, and its requirements studied, weighed, and fulfilled. Superb and irresistible as is the beauty of the first Mashriqu'l-Adhkár of the West, majestic as are its dimensions, unique as is its architecture, and priceless as are the ideals and the aspirations which it symbolizes, it should be regarded, at the present time, as no more than an instrument for a more effective propagation of the Cause and a wider diffusion of its teachings. In this respect it should be viewed in the same light as the administrative institutions of the Faith which are designed as vehicles for the proper dissemination of its ideals, its tenets, and its verities. → true teachings.   65

It is, therefore, to the teaching requirements of the Seven Year Plan that the community of the American believers must henceforth direct their careful and sustained attention. The entire community must, as one man, arise to fulfill them. To teach the Cause of God, to proclaim its truths, to defend its interests, to demonstrate, by words as well as by deeds, its indispensability, its potency, and universality, should at no time be regarded as the exclusive concern or sole privilege of   66

Bahá'í administrative institutions, be they Assemblies, or committees. All must participate, however humble their origin, however limited their experience, however restricted their means, however deficient their education, however pressing their cares and preoccupations, however unfavorable the environment in which they live. *"God,"* Bahá'u'lláh, Himself, has unmistakably revealed, *"hath prescribed unto everyone the duty of teaching His Cause." "Say,"* He further has written, *"Teach ye the Cause of God, O people of Bahá, for God hath prescribed unto everyone the duty of proclaiming His Message, and regardeth it as the most meritorious of all deeds."*

67   A high and exalted position in the ranks of the community, conferring as it does on its holder certain privileges and prerogatives, no doubt invests him with a responsibility that he cannot honorably shirk in his duty to teach and promote the Faith of God. It may, at times, though not invariably, create greater opportunities and furnish better facilities to spread the knowledge of that Faith, and to win supporters to its institutions. It does not, however, under any circumstances, necessarily carry with it the power of exercising greater influence on the minds and hearts of those to whom that Faith is presented. How often—and the early history of the Faith in the land of its birth offers many a striking testimony—have the lowliest adherents of the Faith, unschooled and utterly inexperienced, and with no

standing whatever, and in some cases devoid of intelligence, been capable of winning victories for their Cause, before which the most brilliant achievements of the learned, the wise, and the experienced have paled.

"*Peter*," 'Abdu'l-Bahá has testified, "*according to the history of the Church, was also incapable of keeping count of the days of the week. Whenever he decided to go fishing, he would tie up his weekly food into seven parcels, and every day he would eat one of them, and when he had reached the seventh, he would know that the Sabbath had arrived, and thereupon would observe it.*" If the Son of Man was capable of infusing into apparently so crude and helpless an instrument such potency as to cause, in the words of Bahá'u'lláh, "*the mysteries of wisdom and of utterance to flow out of his mouth,*" and to exalt him above the rest of His disciples, and render him fit to become His successor and the founder of His Church, how much more can the Father, Who is Bahá'u'lláh, empower the most puny and insignificant among His followers to achieve, for the execution of His purpose, such wonders as would dwarf the mightiest achievements of even the first apostle of Jesus Christ!

"*The Báb,*" 'Abdu'l-Bahá, moreover, has written, "*hath said: 'Should a tiny ant desire, in this day, to be possessed of such power as to be able to unravel the abstrusest and most bewildering passages of the Qur'án, its wish will no doubt be fulfilled, inasmuch as the mystery of eternal*

68

69

might vibrates within the innermost being of all created things.' If so helpless a creature can be endowed with so subtle a capacity, how much more efficacious must be the power released through the liberal effusions of the grace of Bahá'u'lláh!"

effective

70   The field is indeed so immense, the period so critical, the Cause so great, the workers so few, the time so short, the privilege so priceless, that no follower of the Faith of Bahá'u'lláh, worthy to bear His name, can afford a moment's hesitation. That God-born Force, irresistible in its sweeping power, incalculable in its potency, unpredictable in its course, mysterious in its workings, and awe-inspiring in its manifestations—a Force which, as the Báb has written, *"vibrates within the innermost being of all created things,"* and which, according to Bahá'u'lláh, has through its *"vibrating influence,"* *"upset the equilibrium of the world and revolutionized its ordered life"*—such a Force, acting even as a two-edged sword, is, under our very eyes, sundering, on the one hand, the age-old ties which for centuries have held together the fabric of civilized society, and is unloosing, on the other, the bonds that still fetter the infant and as yet unemancipated Faith of Bahá'u'lláh. The undreamt-of opportunities offered through the operation of this Force—the American believers must now rise, and fully and courageously exploit them. *"The holy realities of the Concourse on high,"* writes 'Abdu'l-

Angels in the abha Kingdom

Bahá, *"yearn, in this day, in the Most Exalted Paradise, to return unto this world, so that they may be aided to render some service to the threshold of the Abhá Beauty, and arise to demonstrate their servitude to His sacred Threshold."*

A world, dimmed by the steadily dying-out light of 71 religion, heaving with the explosive forces of a blind and triumphant nationalism; scorched with the fires of pitiless persecution, whether racial or religious; deluded by the false theories and doctrines that threaten to supplant the worship of God and the sanctification of His laws; enervated by a rampant and brutal materialism; disintegrating through the corrosive influence of moral and spiritual decadence; and enmeshed in the coils of economic anarchy and strife—such is the spectacle presented to men's eyes, as a result of the sweeping changes which this revolutionizing Force, as yet in the initial stage of its operation, is now producing in the life of the entire planet.

So sad and moving a spectacle, bewildering as it must 72 be to every observer unaware of the purposes, the prophecies, and promises of Bahá'u'lláh, far from casting dismay into the hearts of His followers, or paralyzing their efforts, cannot but deepen their faith, and excite their enthusiastic eagerness to arise and display, in the vast field traced for them by the pen of 'Abdu'l-Bahá, their capacity to play their part in the work of universal redemption proclaimed by Bahá'u'lláh. Every instrument in the administrative machinery which, in the course of several years, they have so laboriously erected must be fully utilized, and subordinated to the end for which it was created. The Temple, that proud embodiment of so rare a spirit of self-sacrifice, must likewise be made to play its part, and contribute its share to the teaching campaign designed to embrace the entire Western Hemisphere.

73   The opportunities which the turmoil of the present age presents, with all the sorrows which it evokes, the fears which it excites, the disillusionment which it produces, the perplexities which it creates, the indignation which it arouses, the revolt which it provokes, the grievances it engenders, the spirit of restless search which it awakens, must, in like manner, be exploited for the purpose of spreading far and wide the knowledge of the redemptive power of the Faith of Bahá'u'lláh, and for enlisting fresh recruits in the ever-swelling army of His followers. So precious an opportunity, so rare a conjunction of favorable circumstances, may never again recur. Now is the time, the appointed time, for the American believers, the vanguard of the hosts of the Most Great Name, to proclaim, through the agencies and channels of a specially designed Administrative Order, their capacity and readiness to rescue a fallen and sore-tried generation that has rebelled against

its God and ignored His warnings, and to offer it that complete security which only the strongholds of their Faith can provide.

The teaching campaign, inaugurated throughout the 74 states of the North American Republic and the Dominion of Canada, acquires, therefore, an importance, and is invested with an urgency, that cannot be overestimated. Launched on its course through the creative energies released by the Will of 'Abdu'l-Bahá, and sweeping across the Western Hemisphere through the propelling force which it is generating, it must, I feel, be carried out in conformity with certain principles, designed to insure its efficient conduct, and to hasten the attainment of its objective.

Those who participate in such a campaign, whether 75 in an organizing capacity, or as workers to whose care the execution of the task itself has been committed, must, as an essential preliminary to the discharge of their duties, thoroughly familiarize themselves with the various aspects of the history and teachings of their Faith. In their efforts to achieve this purpose they must study for themselves, conscientiously and painstakingly, the literature of their Faith, delve into its teachings, assimilate its laws and principles, ponder its admonitions, tenets and purposes, commit to memory certain of its exhortations and prayers, master the essentials of its administration, and keep abreast of its current affairs and latest developments. They must strive to obtain, from sources that are authoritative and unbiased, a sound knowledge of the history and tenets of Islám— the source and background of their Faith—and approach reverently and with a mind purged from preconceived ideas the study of the Qur'án which, apart from the sacred scriptures of the Bábí and Bahá'í Revelations, constitutes the only Book which can be regarded as an absolutely authenticated Repository of the Word of God. They must devote special attention to the investigation of those institutions and circumstances that are directly connected with the origin and birth of their Faith, with the station claimed by its Forerunner, and with the laws revealed by its Author.

76   Having acquired, in their essentials, these prerequisites of success in the teaching field, they must, whenever they contemplate undertaking any specific mission in the countries of Latin America, endeavor, whenever feasible, to acquire a certain proficiency in the languages spoken by the inhabitants of those countries, and a knowledge of their customs, habits, and outlook. *"The teachers going to those parts,"* 'Abdu'l-Bahá, referring in one of the Tablets of the Divine Plan to the Central American Republics, has written, *"must also be familiar with the Spanish language." "A party speaking their languages . . . ,"* He, in another Tablet, has written, *"must turn their faces to and travel through the three*

great Island groups of the Pacific Ocean." "The teachers traveling in different directions," He further states, *"must know the language of the country in which they will enter. For example, a person being proficient in the Japanese language may travel to Japan, or a person knowing the Chinese language may hasten to China, and so forth."*

No participator in this inter-American campaign of teaching must feel that the initiative for any particular activity connected with this work must rest solely with those agencies, whether Assemblies or committees, whose special concern is to promote and facilitate the attainment of this vital objective of the Seven Year Plan. It is the bounden duty of every American believer, as the faithful trustee of 'Abdu'l-Bahá's Divine Plan, to initiate, promote, and consolidate, within the limits fixed by the administrative principles of the Faith, any activity he or she deems fit to undertake for the furtherance of the Plan. Neither the threatening world situation, nor any consideration of lack of material resources, of mental equipment, of knowledge, or of experience—desirable as they are—should deter any prospective pioneer teacher from arising independently, and from setting in motion the forces which, 'Abdu'l-Bahá has repeatedly assured us, will, once released, attract even as a magnet the promised and infallible aid of Bahá'u'lláh. Let him not wait for any directions, or expect any special encouragement, from the elected representatives of his community, nor be deterred by any obstacles which his relatives, or fellow-citizens may be inclined to place in his path, nor mind the censure of his critics or enemies. *"Be unrestrained as the wind,"* is Bahá'u'lláh's counsel to every would-be teacher of His Cause, *"while carrying the Message of Him Who hath caused the dawn of Divine Guidance to break. Consider how the wind, faithful to that which God hath ordained, bloweth upon all regions of the earth, be they inhabited or desolate. Neither the sight of desolation, nor the evidences of prosperity, can either pain or please it. It bloweth in every direction, as bidden by its Creator."* *"And when he determineth to leave his home, for the sake of the Cause of his Lord,"* Bahá'u'lláh, in another passage, referring to such a teacher, has revealed, *"let him put his whole trust in God, as the best provision for his journey, and array himself with the robe of virtue. . . . If he be kindled with the fire of His love, if he forgoeth all created things, the words he uttereth shall set on fire them that hear him."*

78   Having on his own initiative, and undaunted by any hindrances with which either friend or foe may, unwittingly or deliberately, obstruct his path, resolved to arise and respond to the call of teaching, let him carefully consider every avenue of approach which he might utilize in his personal attempts to capture the attention, maintain the interest, and deepen the faith, of those whom he seeks to bring into the fold of his Faith.

Let him survey the possibilities which the particular circumstances in which he lives offer him, evaluate their advantages, and proceed intelligently and systematically to utilize them for the achievement of the object he has in mind. Let him also attempt to devise such methods as association with clubs, exhibitions, and societies, lectures on subjects akin to the teachings and ideals of his Cause such as temperance, morality, social welfare, religious and racial tolerance, economic cooperation, Islám, and Comparative Religion, or participation in social, cultural, humanitarian, charitable, and educational organizations and enterprises which, while safeguarding the integrity of his Faith, will open up to him a multitude of ways and means whereby he can enlist successively the sympathy, the support, and ultimately the allegiance of those with whom he comes in contact. Let him, while such contacts are being made, bear in mind the claims which his Faith is constantly making upon him to preserve its dignity, and station, to safeguard the integrity of its laws and principles, to demonstrate its comprehensiveness and universality, and to defend fearlessly its manifold and vital interests. Let him consider the degree of his hearer's receptivity, and decide for himself the suitability of either the direct or indirect method of teaching, whereby he can impress upon the seeker the vital importance of the Divine Message, and persuade him to throw in his lot with those who have already embraced it. Let him remember the example set by 'Abdu'l-Bahá, and His constant admonition to shower such kindness upon the seeker, and exemplify to such a degree the spirit of the teachings he hopes to instill into him, that the recipient will be spontaneously impelled to identify himself with the Cause embodying such teachings. Let him refrain, at the outset, from insisting on such laws and observances as might impose too severe a strain on the seeker's newly awakened faith, and endeavor to nurse him, patiently, tactfully, and yet determinedly, into full maturity, and aid him to proclaim his unqualified acceptance of whatever has been ordained by Bahá'u'lláh. Let him, as soon as that stage has been attained, introduce him to the body of his fellow-believers, and seek, through constant fellowship and active participation in the local activities of his community, to enable him to contribute his share to the enrichment of its life, the furtherance of its tasks, the consolidations of its interests, and the coordination of its activities with those of its sister communities. Let him not be content until he has infused into his spiritual child so deep a longing as to impel him to arise independently, in his turn, and devote his energies to the quickening of other souls, and the upholding of the laws and principles laid down by his newly adopted Faith.

Let every participator in the continent-wide campaign initiated by the American believers, and particularly those engaged in pioneer work in virgin territories, bear in mind the necessity of keeping in close and
constant touch with those responsible agencies designed
to direct, coordinate, and facilitate the teaching activities of the entire community. Whether it be the body
of their elected national representatives, or its chief
auxiliary institution, the National Teaching Committee, or its subsidiary organs, the regional teaching committees, or the local Spiritual Assemblies and their respective teaching committees, they who labor for the
spread of the Cause of Bahá'u'lláh should, through
constant interchange of ideas, through letters, circulars,
reports, bulletins and other means of communication
with these established instruments designed for the
propagation of the Faith, insure the smooth and speedy
functioning of the teaching machinery of their Administrative Order. Confusion, delay, duplication of efforts,
dissipation of energy will, thereby, be completely avoided, and the mighty flood of the grace of Bahá'u'lláh, flowing abundantly and without the least
obstruction through these essential channels will so
inundate the hearts and souls of men as to enable them
to bring forth the harvest repeatedly predicted by
'Abdu'l-Bahá.

80   Upon every participator in this concerted effort, unprecedented in the annals of the American Bahá'í community, rests the spiritual obligation to make of the mandate of teaching, so vitally binding upon all, the all-pervading concern of his life. In his daily activities and contacts, in all his journeys, whether for business or otherwise, on his holidays and outings, and on any mission he may be called upon to undertake, every bearer of the Message of Bahá'u'lláh should consider it not only an obligation but a privilege to scatter far and wide the seeds of His Faith, and to rest content in the abiding knowledge that whatever be the immediate response to that Message, and however inadequate the vehicle that conveyed it, the power of its Author will, as He sees fit, enable those seeds to germinate, and in circumstances which no one can foresee enrich the harvest which the labor of His followers will gather. If he be member of any Spiritual Assembly let him encourage his Assembly to consecrate a certain part of its time, at each of its sessions, to the earnest and prayerful consideration of such ways and means as may foster the campaign of teaching, or may furnish whatever resources are available for its progress, extension, and consolidation. If he attends his summer school—and everyone without exception is urged to take advantage of attending it—let him consider such an occasion as a welcome and precious opportunity so to enrich,

through lectures, study, and discussion, his knowledge of the fundamentals of his Faith as to be able to transmit, with greater confidence and effectiveness, the Message that has been entrusted to his care. Let him, moreover, seek, whenever feasible, through intercommunity visits to stimulate the zeal for teaching, and to demonstrate to outsiders the zest and alertness of the promoters of his Cause and the organic unity of its institutions.

Let anyone who feels the urge among the participators in this crusade, which embraces all the races, all the republics, classes and denominations of the entire Western Hemisphere, arise, and, circumstances permitting, direct in particular the attention, and win eventually the unqualified adherence, of the Negro, the Indian, the Eskimo, and Jewish races to his Faith. No more laudable and meritorious service can be rendered the Cause of God, at the present hour, than a successful effort to enhance the diversity of the members of the American Bahá'í community by swelling the ranks of the Faith through the enrollment of the members of these races. A blending of these highly differentiated elements of the human race, harmoniously interwoven into the fabric of an all-embracing Bahá'í fraternity, and assimilated through the dynamic processes of a divinely appointed Administrative Order, and contributing each its share to the enrichment and glory of

Bahá'í community life, is surely an achievement the contemplation of which must warm and thrill every Bahá'í heart. *"Consider the flowers of a garden,"* 'Abdu'l-Bahá has written, *"though differing in kind, color, form, and shape, yet, inasmuch as they are refreshed by the waters of one spring, revived by the breath of one wind, invigorated by the rays of one sun, this diversity increaseth their charm, and addeth unto their beauty. How unpleasing to the eye if all the flowers and plants, the leaves and blossoms, the fruits, the branches and the trees of that garden were all of the same shape and color! Diversity of hues, form and shape, enricheth and adorneth the garden, and heighteneth the effect thereof. In like manner, when divers shades of thought, temperament and character, are brought together under the power and influence of one central agency, the beauty and glory of human perfection will be revealed and made manifest. Naught but the celestial potency of the Word of God, which ruleth and transcendeth the realities of all things, is capable of harmonizing the divergent thoughts, sentiments, ideas, and convictions of the children of men."* *"I hope,"* is the wish expressed by 'Abdu'l-Bahá, *"that ye may cause that downtrodden race* [Negro] *to become glorious, and to be joined with the white race to serve the world of man with the utmost sincerity, faithfulness, love and purity."* *"One of the important questions,"* He also has written, *"which affect the unity and the solidarity of mankind is the fel-*

lowship and equality of the white and colored races." "You must attach great importance," writes 'Abdu'l-Bahá in the Tablets of the Divine Plan, *"to the Indians, the original inhabitants of America. For these souls may be likened unto the ancient inhabitants of the Arabian Peninsula, who, prior to the Revelation of Muḥammad, were like savages. When the Muḥammadan Light shone forth in their midst, they became so enkindled that they shed illumination upon the world. Likewise, should these Indians be educated and properly guided, there can be no doubt that through the Divine teachings they will become so enlightened that the whole earth will be illumined." "If it is possible,"* 'Abdu'l-Bahá has also written, *"send ye teachers to other portions of Canada; likewise, dispatch ye teachers to Greenland and the home of the Eskimos." "God willing,"* He further has written in those same Tablets, *"the call of the Kingdom may reach the ears of the Eskimos. . . . Should you display an effort, so that the fragrances of God may be diffused among the Eskimos, its effect will be very great and far-reaching." "Praise be to God,"* writes 'Abdu'l-Bahá, *"that whatsoever hath been announced in the Blessed Tablets unto the Israelites, and the things explicitly written in the letters of 'Abdu'l-Bahá, are all being fulfilled. Some have come to pass; others will be revealed in the future. The Ancient Beauty hath in His sacred Tablets explicitly written that the day of their abasement is over. His bounty will overshadow them, and this race will day by day progress, and be delivered from its age-long obscurity and degradation."*

82   Let those who are holding administrative positions in their capacity as members of either the National Spiritual Assembly, or of the national, the regional, or local teaching committees, continually bear in mind the vital and urgent necessity of insuring, within as short a time as possible, the formation, in the few remaining states of the North American Republic and the provinces of the Dominion of Canada, of groups, however small and rudimentary, and of providing every facility within their power to enable these newly formed nuclei to evolve, swiftly and along sound lines, into properly functioning, self-sufficient, and recognized Assemblies. To the laying of such foundations, the erection of such outposts—a work admittedly arduous, yet sorely needed and highly inspiring—the individual members of the American Bahá'í community must lend their unstinted, continual, and enthusiastic support. Wise as may be the measures which their elected representatives may devise, however practical and well conceived the plans they formulate, such measures and plans can never yield any satisfactory results unless a sufficient number of pioneers have determined to make the necessary sacrifices, and to volunteer to carry these projects into effect. To implant, once and for all, the banner of Bahá'u'lláh in the heart of these

virgin territories, to erect the structural basis of His Administrative Order in their cities and villages, and to establish a firm and permanent anchorage for its institutions in the minds and hearts of their inhabitants, constitute, I firmly believe, the first and most significant step in the successive stages through which the teaching campaign, inaugurated under the Seven Year Plan, must pass. Whereas the external ornamentation of the Mashriqu'l-Adhkár, under this same Plan, has now entered the final phase in its development, the teaching campaign is still in its initial stages, and is far from having extended effectively its ramifications to either these virgin territories, or to those Republics that are situated in the South American continent. The effort required is prodigious, the conditions under which these preliminary establishments are to be made are often unattractive and unfavorable, the workers who are in a position to undertake such tasks limited, and the resources they can command meager and inadequate. And yet, how often has the pen of Bahá'u'lláh assured us that *"should a man, all alone, arise in the name of Bahá, and put on the armor of His love, him will the Almighty cause to be victorious, though the forces of earth and heaven be arrayed against him."* Has He not written: *"By God, besides Whom is none other God! Should anyone arise for the triumph of our Cause, him will God render victorious though tens of thousands of enemies be leagued against him. And if his love for me wax stronger, God will estab-lish his ascendancy over all the powers of earth and heaven." "Consider the work of former generations,"* 'Abdu'l-Bahá has written; *"During the lifetime of Jesus Christ the believing, firm souls were few and numbered, but the heavenly blessings descended so plentifully that in a number of years countless souls entered beneath the shadow of the Gospel. God has said in the Qur'án: 'One grain will bring forth seven sheaves, and every sheaf shall contain one hundred grains.' In other words, one grain will become seven hundred; and if God so wills He will double these also. It has often happened that one blessed soul has become the cause of the guidance of a nation. Now we must not consider our ability and capacity, nay rather we must fix our gaze upon the favors and bounties of God, in these days, Who has made of the drop a sea, and of the atom a sun."* Let those who resolve to be the first to hoist the standard of such a Cause, under such conditions, and in such territories, nourish their souls with the sustaining power of these words, and, *"putting on the armor of His love,"* a love which must *"wax stron-ger"* as they persevere in their lonesome task, arise to adorn with the tale of their deeds the most brilliant pages ever written in their country's spiritual history.

83   *"Although,"* 'Abdu'l-Bahá, in the Tablets of the Di-vine Plan, has written, *"in most of the states and cities of the United States, praise be to God, His fragrances are*

diffused, and souls unnumbered are turning their faces and advancing toward the Kingdom of God, yet in some of the states the Standard of Unity is not yet upraised as it should be, nor are the mysteries of the Holy Books, such as the Bible, the Gospel, and the Qur'án, unraveled. Through the concerted efforts of all the friends the Standard of Unity must needs be unfurled in those states, and the Divine teachings promoted, so that these states may also receive their portion of the heavenly bestowals and a share of the Most Great Guidance." "The future of the Dominion of Canada," He, in another Tablet of the Divine Plan, has asserted, *"is very great, and the events connected with it infinitely glorious. The eye of God's loving-kindness will be turned towards it, and it shall become the manifestation of the favors of the All-Glorious." "Again I repeat,"* He, in that same Tablet reaffirms His previous statement, *"that the future of Canada, whether from a material or a spiritual standpoint, is very great."*

No sooner is this initial step taken, involving as it does the formation of at least one nucleus in each of these virgin states and provinces in the North American continent, than the machinery for a tremendous intensification of Bahá'í concerted effort must be set in motion, the purpose of which should be the reinforcement of the noble exertions which only a few isolated believers are now making for the awakening of the nations of Latin America to the Call of Bahá'u'lláh. 84

Not until this second phase of the teaching campaign, under the Seven Year Plan, has been entered can the campaign be regarded as fully launched, or the Plan itself as having attained the most decisive stage in its evolution. So powerful will be the effusions of Divine grace that will be poured forth upon a valiant community that has already in the administrative sphere erected, in all the glory of its exterior ornamentation, its chief Edifice, and in the teaching field raised aloft, in every state and province, in the North American continent the banner of its Faith—so great will be these effusions that its members will find themselves overpowered by the evidences of their regenerative power.

85   The Inter-America Committee must, at such a stage, nay even before it is entered, rise to the level of its opportunities, and display a vigor, a consecration, and enterprise as will be commensurate with the responsibilities it has shouldered. It should not, for a moment, be forgotten that Central and Southern America embrace no less than twenty independent nations, constituting approximately one-third of the entire number of the world's sovereign states, and are destined to play an increasingly important part in the shaping of the world's future destiny. With the world contracting into a neighborhood, and the fortunes of its races, nations and peoples becoming inextricably interwoven, the remoteness of these states of the Western Hemisphere is

vanishing, and the latent possibilities in each of them are becoming increasingly apparent.

When this second stage in the progressive unfold-   86
ment of teaching activities and enterprises, under the Seven Year Plan, is reached, and the machinery required for its prosecution begins to operate, the American believers, the stout-hearted pioneers of this mighty movement, must, guided by the unfailing light of Bahá'u'lláh, and in strict accordance with the Plan laid out by 'Abdu'l-Bahá, and acting under the direction of their National Spiritual Assembly, and assured of the aid of the Inter-America Committee, launch an offensive against the powers of darkness, of corruption, and of ignorance, an offensive that must extend to the uttermost end of the Southern continent, and embrace within its scope each of the twenty nations that compose it.

Let some, at this very moment, gird up the loins of   87
their endeavor, flee their native towns, cities, and states, forsake their country, and, *"putting their whole trust in God as the best provision for their journey,"* set their faces, and direct their steps towards those distant climes, those virgin fields, those unsurrendered cities, and bend their energies to capture the citadels of men's hearts—hearts, which, as Bahá'u'lláh has written, *"the hosts of Revelation and of utterance can subdue."* Let them not tarry until such time as their fellow-laborers will have passed

the first stage in their campaign of teaching, but let them rather, from this very hour, arise to usher in the opening phase of what will come to be regarded as one of the most glorious chapters in the international history of their Faith. Let them, at the very outset, *"teach their own selves, that their speech may attract the hearts of their hearers."* Let them regard the triumph of their Faith as their *"supreme objective."* Let them not *"consider the largeness or smallness of the receptacle"* that carries the measure of grace that God poureth forth in this age. Let them *"disencumber themselves of all attachment to this world and the vanities thereof,"* and, with that spirit of detachment which 'Abdu'l-Bahá exemplified and wished them to emulate, bring these diversified peoples and countries to the remembrance of God and His supreme Manifestation. Let His love be a *"storehouse of treasure for their souls,"* on the day when *"every pillar shall tremble, when the very skins of men shall creep, when all eyes shall stare up with terror."* Let their *"souls be aglow with the flame of the undying Fire that burneth in the midmost heart of the world, in such wise that the waters of the universe shall be powerless to cool down its ardor."* Let them be *"unrestrained as the wind"* which *"neither the sight of desolation nor the evidences of prosperity can either pain or please."* Let them *"unloose their tongues and proclaim unceasingly His Cause."* Let them *"proclaim that which the Most Great Spirit will inspire them to utter in the service of the Cause of their Lord."* Let them *"beware lest they contend with anyone, nay strive to make him aware of the truth with kindly manner and most convincing exhortation."* Let them *"wholly for the sake of God proclaim His Message, and with that same spirit accept whatever response their words may evoke in their hearers."* Let them not, for one moment, forget that the *"Faithful Spirit shall strengthen them through its power,"* and that *"a company of His chosen angels shall go forth with them, as bidden by Him Who is the Almighty, the All-Wise."* Let them ever bear in mind *"how great is the blessedness that awaiteth them that have attained the honor of serving the Almighty,"* and remember that *"such a service is indeed the prince of all goodly deeds, and the ornament of every goodly act."*

And, finally, let these soul-stirring words of Bahá'u'lláh, as they pursue their course throughout the length and breadth of the southern American continent, be ever ready on their lips, a solace to their hearts, a light on their path, a companion in their loneliness, and a daily sustenance in their journeys: *"O wayfarer in the path of God! Take thou thy portion of the ocean of His grace, and deprive not thyself of the things that lie hidden in its depths. . . . A dewdrop out of this ocean would, if shed upon all that are in the heavens and on earth, suffice to enrich them with the bounty of God, the Almighty, the All-Knowing, the All-Wise. With the hands of renuncia-*

tion draw forth from its life-giving waters, and sprinkle therewith all created things, that they may be cleansed from all man-made limitations, and may approach the mighty seat of God, this hallowed and resplendent Spot. Be not grieved if thou performest it thyself alone. Let God be all-sufficient for thee. . . . Proclaim the Cause of thy Lord unto all who are in the heavens and on the earth. Should any man respond to thy call, lay bare before him the pearls of the wisdom of the Lord, thy God, which His Spirit hath sent down upon thee, and be thou of them that truly believe. And should anyone reject thy offer, turn thou away from him, and put thy trust and confidence in the Lord of all worlds. By the righteousness of God! Whoso openeth his lips in this day, and maketh mention of the name of his Lord, the hosts of Divine inspiration shall descend upon him from the heaven of my name, the All-Knowing, the All-Wise. On him shall also descend the Concourse on high, each bearing aloft a chalice of pure light. Thus hath it been foreordained in the realm of God's Revelation, by the behest of Him Who is the All-Glorious, the Most Powerful."

89   Let these words of 'Abdu'l-Bahá, gleaned from the Tablets of the Divine Plan, ring likewise in their ears, as they go forth, assured and unafraid, on His mission: *"O ye apostles of Bahá'u'lláh! May my life be sacrificed for you! . . . Behold the portals which Bahá'u'lláh hath opened before you! Consider how exalted and lofty is the*

station you are destined to attain; how unique the favors with which you have been endowed." "My thoughts are turned towards you, and my heart leaps within me at your mention. Could ye know how my soul gloweth with your love, so great a happiness would flood your hearts as to cause you to become enamored with each other." "The full measure of your success is as yet unrevealed, its significance still unapprehended. Erelong ye will, with your own eyes, witness how brilliantly every one of you, even as a shining star, will radiate in the firmament of your country the light of Divine Guidance, and will bestow upon its people the glory of an everlasting life." "I fervently hope that in the near future the whole earth may be stirred and shaken by the results of your achievements." "The Almighty will no doubt grant you the help of His grace, will invest you with the tokens of His might, and will endue your souls with the sustaining power of His holy Spirit." "Be not concerned with the smallness of your numbers, neither be oppressed by the multitude of an unbelieving world. . . . Exert yourselves; your mission is unspeakably glorious. Should success crown your enterprise, America will assuredly evolve into a center from which waves of spiritual power will emanate, and the throne of the Kingdom of God will, in the plenitude of its majesty and glory, be firmly established."

It should be remembered that the carrying out of 90 the Seven Year Plan involves, insofar as the teaching work is concerned, no more than the formation of at least one center in each of the Central and South American Republics. The hundredth anniversary of the birth of the Faith of Bahá'u'lláh should witness, if the Plan already launched is to meet with success, the laying, in each of these countries, of a foundation, however rudimentary, on which the rising generation of the American believers may, in the opening years of the second century of the Bahá'í era, be able to build. Theirs will be the task, in the course of successive decades, to extend and reinforce those foundations, and to supply the necessary guidance, assistance, and encouragement that will enable the widely scattered groups of believers in those countries to establish independent and properly constituted local Assemblies, and thereby erect the framework of the Administrative Order of their Faith. The erection of such a framework is primarily the responsibility of those whom the community of the North American believers have converted to the Divine Message. It is a task which must involve, apart from the immediate obligation of enabling every group to evolve into a local Assembly, the setting up of the entire machinery of the Administrative Order in conformity with the spiritual and administrative principles governing the life and activities of every established Bahá'í community throughout the world. No departure from these cardinal and clearly enunciated principles, embodied and preserved in Bahá'í national and local constitutions, common to all Bahá'í communities, can under any circumstances be tolerated. This, however, is a task that concerns those who, at a later period, must arise to further a work which, to all intents and purposes, has not yet been effectively started.

To pave the way, in a more systematic manner, for the laying of the necessary foundation on which such permanent national and local institutions can be reared and securely established is a task that will very soon demand the concentrated attention of the prosecutors of the Seven Year Plan. No sooner has their immediate obligation in connection with the opening up of the few remaining territories in the United States and Canada been discharged, than a carefully laid-out plan should be conceived, aiming at the establishment of such a foundation. As already stated, the provision for these vast, preliminary undertakings, the scope of which must embrace the entire area occupied by the Central and South American Republics, constitutes the very core, and must ultimately decide the fate, of the teaching campaign conducted under the Seven Year Plan. Upon this campaign must depend not only the effectual discharge of the solemn obligations undertaken in connection with the present Plan, but also the progressive unfoldment of the subsequent stages essential to the realization of 'Abdu'l-Bahá's vision of the part the

American believers are to play in the worldwide propagation of their Cause.

92   These undertakings, preliminary as they are to the strenuous and organized labors by which future generations of believers in the Latin countries must distinguish themselves, require, in turn, without a moment's delay, on the part of the National Spiritual Assembly and of both the National Teaching and Inter-America Committees, painstaking investigations preparatory to the sending of settlers and itinerant teachers, whose privilege will be to raise the call of the New Day in a new continent.

93   I can only, in my desire to be of some service to those who are to assume such tremendous responsibilities, and to suffer such self-denial, attempt to offer a few helpful suggestions which, I trust, will facilitate the accomplishment of the great work to be achieved in the very near future. To this work, that must constitute an historical landmark of first-class importance when completed, the energies of the entire community must be resolutely consecrated. The number of Bahá'í teachers, be they settlers or travelers, must be substantially increased. The material resources to be placed at their disposal must be multiplied, and efficiently administered. The literature with which they should be equipped must be vastly augmented. The publicity that should aid them in the distribution of

such literature should be extended, centrally organized, and vigorously conducted. The possibilities latent in these countries should be diligently exploited, and systematically developed. The various obstacles raised by the widely varying political and social conditions obtaining in these countries should be closely surveyed and determinedly surmounted. In a word, no opportunity should be neglected, and no effort spared, to lay as broad and solid a basis as possible for the progress and development of the greatest teaching enterprise ever launched by the American Bahá'í community.

The careful translation of such important Bahá'í 94 writings as are related to the history, the teachings, or the Administrative Order of the Faith, and their wide and systematic dissemination, in vast quantities, and throughout as many of these Republics as possible, and in languages that are most suitable and needed, would appear to be the chief and most urgent measure to be taken simultaneously with the arrival of the pioneer workers in those fields. *"Books and pamphlets,"* writes 'Abdu'l-Bahá in one of the Tablets of the Divine Plan, *"must be either translated or composed in the languages of these countries and islands, to be circulated in every part and in all directions."* In countries where no objections can be raised by the civil authorities or any influential circles, this measure should be reinforced by the publication, in various organs of the Press, of carefully worded articles and letters, designed to impress upon the general public certain features of the stirring history of the Faith, and the range and character of its teachings.

95   Every laborer in those fields, whether as traveling teacher or settler, should, I feel, make it his chief and constant concern to mix, in a friendly manner, with all sections of the population, irrespective of class, creed, nationality, or color, to familiarize himself with their ideas, tastes, and habits, to study the approach best suited to them, to concentrate, patiently and tactfully, on a few who have shown marked capacity and receptivity, and to endeavor, with extreme kindness, to implant such love, zeal, and devotion in their hearts as to enable them to become in turn self-sufficient and independent promoters of the Faith in their respective localities. *"Consort with all men, O people of Bahá,"* is Bahá'u'lláh's admonition, *"in a spirit of friendliness and fellowship. If ye be aware of a certain truth, if ye possess a jewel, of which others are deprived, share it with them in a language of utmost kindliness and goodwill. If it be accepted, if it fulfill its purpose, your object is attained. If anyone should refuse it, leave him unto himself, and beseech God to guide him. Beware lest ye deal unkindly with him. A kindly tongue is the lodestone of the hearts of men. It is the bread of the spirit, it clotheth the words*

with meaning, it is the fountain of the light of wisdom and understanding."

An effort, moreover, can and should be made, not only by representative Bahá'í bodies, but also by prospective teachers, as well as by other individual believers, deprived of the privilege of visiting those shores or of settling on that continent, to seize every opportunity that presents itself to make the acquaintance, and awaken the genuine interest, of such people who are either citizens of these countries, or are in any way connected with them, whatever be their interests or profession. Through the kindness shown them, or any literature which may be given them, or any connection which they may establish with them, the American believers can thereby sow such seeds in their hearts as might, in future circumstances, germinate and yield the most unexpected results. Care, however, should, at all times, be exercised, lest in their eagerness to further the international interests of the Faith they frustrate their purpose, and turn away, through any act that might be misconstrued as an attempt to proselytize and bring undue pressure upon them, those whom they wish to win over to their Cause. 96

I would particularly direct my appeal to those American believers, sore-pressed as they are by the manifold, the urgent, and ever-increasing issues that confront 97 them at the present hour, who may find it possible, whatever be their calling or employment, whether as businessmen, school teachers, lawyers, doctors, writers, office workers, and the like, to establish permanently their residence in such countries as may offer them a reasonable prospect of earning the means of livelihood. They will by their action be relieving the continually increasing pressure on their Teaching Fund, which in view of its restricted dimensions must provide, when not otherwise available, the traveling and other expenses to be incurred in connection with the development of this vast undertaking. Should they find it impossible to take advantage of so rare and sacred a privilege, let them, mindful of the words of Bahá'u'lláh, determine, each according to the means at his or her disposal, to appoint a deputy who, on that believer's behalf, will arise and carry out so noble an enterprise. *"Center your energies,"* are Bahá'u'lláh's words, *"in the propagation of the Faith of God. Whoso is worthy of so high a calling, let him arise and promote it. Whoso is unable, it is his duty to appoint him who will, in his stead, proclaim this Revelation, whose power hath caused the foundations of the mightiest structures to quake, every mountain to be crushed into dust, and every soul to be dumbfounded."*

98 As to those who have been able to leave their homes and country, and to serve in those regions, whether

temporarily or permanently, a special duty, which must continually be borne in mind, devolves upon them. It should be one of their chief aims to keep, on the one hand, in constant touch with the National Committee specifically entrusted with the promotion of their work, and to cooperate, on the other, by every possible means and in the utmost harmony, with their fellow-believers in those countries, whatever the field in which they labor, whatever their standing, ability, or experience. Through the performance of their first duty they will derive the necessary stimulus and obtain the necessary guidance that will enable them to prosecute effectively their mission, and will also, through their regular reports to that committee, be imparting to the general body of their fellow-believers the news of the latest developments in their activities. By fulfilling their other duty, they will insure the smooth efficiency, facilitate the progress, and avert any untoward incidents that might handicap the development of their common enterprise. The maintenance of close contact and harmonious relationships between the Inter-America Committee, entrusted with the immediate responsibility of organizing such a far-reaching enterprise, and the privileged pioneers who are actually executing that enterprise, and extending its ramifications far and wide, as well as among these pioneers themselves, would set, apart from its immediate advantages, a worthy and inspiring example to generations still yet to be born who are to carry on, with all its increasing complexities, the work which is being initiated at present.

99   It would, no doubt, be of exceptional importance and value, particularly in these times when the various restrictions imposed in those countries make it difficult for a considerable number of Bahá'í pioneers to establish their residence and earn their livelihood in those states, if certain ones among the believers, whose income, however slender, provides them with the means of an independent existence, would so arrange their affairs as to be able to reside indefinitely in those countries. The sacrifices involved, the courage, faith, and perseverance it demands, are no doubt very great. Their value, however, can never be properly assessed at the present time, and the limitless reward which they who demonstrate them will receive can never be adequately depicted. *"They that have forsaken their country,"* is Bahá'u'lláh's own testimony, *"for the purpose of teaching Our Cause—these shall the Faithful Spirit strengthen through its power. . . . By My life! No act, however great, can compare with it, except such deeds as have been ordained by God, the All-Powerful, the Most Mighty. Such a service is indeed the prince of all goodly deeds, and the ornament of every goodly act."* Such a reward, it should be noted, is not to be regarded as purely an abstract blessing confined to the future life, but also as a tan-

gible benefit which such courage, faith and perseverance can alone confer in this material world. The solid
achievements, spiritual as well as administrative, which
in the far-away continent of Australasia, and more recently in Bulgaria, representative believers from both
Canada and the United States have accomplished, proclaim in terms unmistakable the nature of those prizes
which, even in this world, such sterling heroism is
bound to win. *"Whoso,"* Bahá'u'lláh, in a memorable
passage, extolling those of His loved ones who have
*"journeyed through the countries in His Name and for His
praise,"* has written, *"hath attained their presence will
glory in their meeting, and all that dwell in every land
will be illumined by their memory."*

I am moved, at this juncture, as I am reminded of   100
the share which, ever since the inception of the Faith
in the West, the handmaidens of Bahá'u'lláh, as distinguished from the men, have had in opening up, single-
handed, so many, such diversified, and widely scattered
countries over the whole surface of the globe, not only
to pay a tribute to such apostolic fervor as is truly reminiscent of those heroic men who were responsible for
the birth of the Faith of Bahá'u'lláh, but also to stress
the significance of such a preponderating share which
the women of the West have had and are having in the
establishment of His Faith throughout the whole world.
"Among the miracles," 'Abdu'l-Bahá Himself has testified,

"which distinguish this sacred Dispensation is this, that women have evinced a greater boldness than men when enlisted in the ranks of the Faith." So great and splendid a testimony applies in particular to the West, and though it has received thus far abundant and convincing confirmation must, as the years roll away, be further reinforced, as the American believers usher in the most glorious phase of their teaching activities under the Seven Year Plan. The *"boldness"* which, in the words of 'Abdu'l-Bahá, has characterized their accomplishments in the past must suffer no eclipse as they stand on the threshold of still greater and nobler accomplishments. Nay rather, it must, in the course of time and throughout the length and breadth of the vast and virgin territories of Latin America, be more convincingly demonstrated, and win for the beloved Cause victories more stirring than any it has as yet achieved.

101   To the Bahá'í youth of America, moreover, I feel a word should be addressed in particular, as I survey the possibilities which a campaign of such gigantic proportions has to offer to the eager and enterprising spirit that so powerfully animates them in the service of the Cause of Bahá'u'lláh. Though lacking in experience and faced with insufficient resources, yet the adventurous spirit which they possess, and the vigor, the alertness, and optimism they have thus far so consistently shown, qualify them to play an active part in arousing the in-

terest, and in securing the allegiance, of their fellow youth in those countries. No greater demonstration can be given to the peoples of both continents of the youthful vitality and the vibrant power animating the life, and the institutions of the nascent Faith of Bahá'u'lláh than an intelligent, persistent, and effective participation of the Bahá'í youth, of every race, nationality, and class, in both the teaching and administrative spheres of Bahá'í activity. Through such a participation the critics and enemies of the Faith, watching with varying degrees of skepticism and resentment, the evolutionary processes of the Cause of God and its institutions, can best be convinced of the indubitable truth that such a Cause is intensely alive, is sound to its very core, and its destinies in safe keeping. I hope, and indeed pray, that such a participation may not only redound to the glory, the power, and the prestige of the Faith, but may also react so powerfully on the spiritual lives, and galvanize to such an extent the energies of the youthful members of the Bahá'í community, as to empower them to display, in a fuller measure, their inherent capacities, and to unfold a further stage in their spiritual evolution under the shadow of the Faith of Bahá'u'lláh.

Faithful to the provisions of the Charter laid down by the pen of 'Abdu'l-Bahá, I feel it my duty to draw the special attention of those to whom it has been en-
102

trusted to the urgent needs of, and the special position enjoyed by, the Republic of Panama, both in view of its relative proximity to the heart and center of the Faith in North America, and of its geographical position as the link between two continents. *"All the above countries,"* 'Abdu'l-Bahá, referring to the Latin States in one of the Tablets of the Divine Plan, has written, *"have importance, but especially the Republic of Panama, wherein the Atlantic and Pacific Oceans come together through the Panama Canal. It is a center for travel and passage from America to other continents of the world, and in the future it will gain most great importance."* *"Likewise,"* He again has written, *"ye must give great attention to the Republic of Panama, for in that point the Occident and the Orient find each other united through the Panama Canal, and it is also situated between the two great oceans. That place will become very important in the future. The teachings, once established there, will unite the East and the West, the North and the South."* So privileged a position surely demands the special and prompt attention of the American Bahá'í community. With the Republic of Mexico already opened up to the Faith, and with a Spiritual Assembly properly constituted in its capital city, the southward penetration of the Faith of Bahá'u'lláh into a neighboring country is but a natural and logical step, and should, it is to be hoped, prove to be not a difficult one. No efforts should be spared, and no sacrifice be deemed too great, to establish even though it be a very small group in a Republic occupying, both spiritually and geographically, so strategic a position—a group which, in view of the potency with which the words of 'Abdu'l-Bahá have already endowed it, cannot but draw to itself, as soon as it is formed, the outpouring grace of the Abhá Kingdom, and evolve with such marvelous swiftness as to excite the wonder and the admiration of even those who have already witnessed such stirring evidences of the force and power of the Faith of Bahá'u'lláh. Preference, no doubt, should be given by all would-be pioneers, as well as by the members of the Inter-America Committee, to the spiritual needs of this privileged Republic, though every effort should, at the same time, be exerted to introduce the Faith, however tentatively, to the Republics of Guatemala, Honduras, El Salvador, Nicaragua, and Costa Rica which would link it, in an unbroken chain, with its mother Assemblies in the North American continent. Obstacles, however formidable, should be surmounted, the resources of the Bahá'í treasury should be liberally expended on its behalf, and the ablest and most precious exertions should be consecrated to the cause of its awakening. The erection of yet another outpost of the Faith, in its heart, will constitute, I firmly believe, a landmark in the history of the Formative Period of the Faith of Bahá'u'lláh in the New World. It will create limitless opportunities, galvanize the efforts, and reinvigorate the life, of those who will have accomplished this feat, and infuse immense courage and boundless joy into the hearts of the isolated groups and individuals in the neighboring and distant Republics, and exert intangible yet powerful spiritual influences on the life and future development of its people.

103   Such, dearly beloved friends, is the vista that stretches before the eyes, and challenges the resources, of the American Bahá'í community in these, the concluding years of the First Century of the Bahá'í Era. Such are the qualities and qualifications demanded of them for the proper discharge of their responsibilities and duties. Such are the requirements, the possibilities, and the objectives of the Plan that claims every ounce of their energy. Who knows but that these few remaining, fast-fleeting years, may not be pregnant with events of unimaginable magnitude, with ordeals more severe than any that humanity has as yet experienced, with conflicts more devastating than any which have preceded them. Dangers, however sinister, must, at no time, dim the radiance of their new-born faith. Strife and confusion, however bewildering, must never befog their vision. Tribulations, however afflictive, must never shatter their resolve. Denunciations, however

clamorous, must never sap their loyalty. Upheavals, however cataclysmic, must never deflect their course. The present Plan, embodying the budding hopes of a departed Master, must be pursued, relentlessly pursued, whatever may befall them in the future, however distracting the crises that may agitate their country or the world. Far from yielding in their resolve, far from growing oblivious of their task, they should, at no time, however much buffeted by circumstances, forget that the synchronization of such world-shaking crises with the progressive unfoldment and fruition of their divinely appointed task is itself the work of Providence, the design of an inscrutable Wisdom, and the purpose of an all-compelling Will, a Will that directs and controls, in its own mysterious way, both the fortunes of the Faith and the destinies of men. Such simultaneous processes of rise and of fall, of integration and of disintegration, of order and chaos, with their continuous and reciprocal reactions on each other, are but aspects of a greater Plan, one and indivisible, whose Source is God, whose author is Bahá'u'lláh, the theater of whose operations is the entire planet, and whose ultimate objectives are the unity of the human race and the peace of all mankind.

Reflections such as these should steel the resolve of   104
the entire Bahá'í community, should dissipate their forebodings, and arouse them to rededicate themselves

to every single provision of that Divine Charter whose outline has been delineated for them by the pen of 'Abdu'l-Bahá. The Seven Year Plan, as already stated, is but the initial stage, a stepping-stone to the unfoldment of the implications of this Charter. The impulse, originally generated through the movement of that pen, and which is now driving forward, with increasing momentum, the machinery of the Seven Year Plan, must, in the opening years of the next century, be further accelerated, and impel the American Bahá'í community to launch further stages in the unfoldment of the Divine Plan, stages that will carry it far beyond the shores of the Northern Hemisphere, into lands and among peoples where that community's noblest acts of heroism are to be performed.

105   Let anyone inclined to doubt the course which this enviable community is destined to follow, turn to and meditate upon these words of 'Abdu'l-Bahá, enshrined, for all time, in the Tablets of the Divine Plan, and addressed to the entire community of the believers of the United States and Canada: *"The full measure of your success,"* He informs them, *"is as yet unrevealed, its significance still unapprehended. Erelong, ye will, with your own eyes, witness how brilliantly every one of you, even as a shining star, will radiate, in the firmament of your country, the light of Divine Guidance, and will bestow upon its people the glory of an everlasting life. . . .*

The range of your future achievements still remains un-disclosed. I fervently hope that in the near future the whole earth may be stirred and shaken by the results of your achievements. The hope, therefore, which 'Abdu'l-Bahá cherishes for you is that the same success which has at-tended your efforts in America may crown your endeavors in other parts of the world, that through you the fame of the Cause of God may be diffused throughout the East and the West, and the advent of the Kingdom of the Lord of Hosts be proclaimed in all the five continents of the globe." "The moment," He most significantly adds, *"this Divine Message is carried forward by the American be-lievers from the shores of America, and is propagated throughout the continents of Europe, of Asia, of Africa, and of Australasia, and as far as the islands of the Pacific, this community will find itself securely established upon the throne of an everlasting dominion. Then will all the peoples of the world witness that this community is spiri-tually illumined and divinely guided. Then will the whole earth resound with the praises of its majesty and greatness."*

No reader of these words, so vibrant with promises that not even the triumphant consummation of the Seven Year Plan can fulfill, can expect a community that has been raised so high, and endowed so richly, to remain content with any laurels it may win in the im-mediate future. To rest upon such laurels would in-

106

deed be tantamount to a betrayal of the trust placed in that community by 'Abdu'l-Bahá. To cut short the chain of victories that must lead it on to that supreme triumph when *"the whole earth may be stirred and shaken"* by the results of its achievements would shatter His hopes. To vacillate, and fail to *"propagate through the continents of Europe, of Asia, of Africa, and of Australasia, and as far as the islands of the Pacific"* a Message so magnificently proclaimed by it in the American continent would deprive it of the privilege of being *"securely established upon the throne of an everlasting dominion."* To forfeit the honor of proclaiming *"the advent of the Kingdom of the Lord of Hosts"* in *"all the five continents of the globe"* would silence those *"praises of its majesty and greatness"* that otherwise would echo throughout *"the whole earth."*

107   Such vacillation, failure, or neglect, the American believers, the ambassadors of the Faith of Bahá'u'lláh, will, I am firmly convinced, never permit. Such a trust will never be betrayed, such hopes can never be shattered, such a privilege will never be forfeited, nor will such praises remain unuttered. Nay rather the present generation of this blessed, this repeatedly blessed, community will go from strength to strength, and will hand on, as the first century draws to a close, to the generations that must succeed it in the second the torch of Divine Guidance, undimmed by the tempestuous

winds that must blow upon it, that they in turn, faithful to the wish and mandate of 'Abdu'l-Bahá, may carry that torch, with that self-same vigor, fidelity, and enthusiasm, to the darkest and remotest corners of the earth.

Dearly beloved friends! I can do no better, eager as I am to extend to every one of you any assistance in my power that may enable you to discharge more effectively your divinely appointed, continually multiplying duties, than to direct your special attention, at this decisive hour, to these immortal passages, gleaned in part from the great mass of Bahá'u'lláh's unpublished and untranslated writings. Whether in His revelation of the station and functions of His loved ones, or His eulogies of the greatness of His Cause, or His emphasis on the paramount importance of teaching, or the dangers which He foreshadows, the counsels He imparts, the warnings He utters, the vistas He discloses, and the assurances and promises He gives, these dynamic and typical examples of Bahá'u'lláh's sublime utterance, each having a direct bearing on the tasks which actually face or lie ahead of the American Bahá'í community, cannot fail to produce on the minds and hearts of any one of its members, who approaches them with befitting humility and detachment, such powerful reactions as to illuminate his entire being and intensify tremendously his daily exertions.

109   "O friends! Be not careless of the virtues with which ye
have been endowed, neither be neglectful of your high
destiny. . . . Ye are the stars of the heaven of understanding, the breeze that stirreth at the break of day, the soft-
flowing waters upon which must depend the very life of
all men, the letters inscribed upon His sacred scroll." "O
people of Bahá! Ye are the breezes of spring that are wafted
over the world. Through you We have adorned the world
of being with the ornament of the knowledge of the Most
Merciful. Through you the countenance of the world hath
been wreathed in smiles, and the brightness of His light
shone forth. Cling ye to the Cord of steadfastness, in such
wise that all vain imaginings may utterly vanish. Speed ye
forth from the horizon of power, in the name of your
Lord, the Unconstrained, and announce unto His servants,
with wisdom and eloquence, the tidings of this Cause,
whose splendor hath been shed upon the world of being.
Beware lest anything withhold you from observing the
things prescribed unto you by the Pen of Glory, as it moved
over His Tablet with sovereign majesty and might. Great
is the blessedness of him that hath hearkened to its shrill
voice, as it was raised, through the power of truth, before
all who are in heaven and all who are on earth. . . . O
people of Bahá! The river that is Life indeed hath flowed
for your sakes. Quaff ye in My name, despite them that
have disbelieved in God, the Lord of Revelation. We have
made you to be the hands of Our Cause. Render ye victo-

rious this Wronged One, Who hath been sore-tried in the hands of the workers of iniquity. He, verily, will aid everyone that aideth Him, and will remember everyone that remembereth Him. To this beareth witness this Tablet that hath shed the splendor of the loving-kindness of your Lord, the All-Glorious, the All-Compelling." "Blessed are the people of Bahá! God beareth Me witness! They are the solace of the eye of creation. Through them the universes have been adorned, and the Preserved Tablet embellished. They are the ones who have sailed on the ark of complete independence, with their faces set towards the Dayspring of Beauty. How great is their blessedness that they have attained unto what their Lord, the Omniscient, the All-Wise, hath willed. Through their light the heavens have been adorned, and the faces of those that have drawn nigh unto Him made to shine." "By the sorrows which afflict the beauty of the All-Glorious! Such is the station ordained for the true believer that if to an extent smaller than a needle's eye the glory of that station were to be unveiled to mankind, every beholder would be consumed away in his longing to attain it. For this reason it hath been decreed that in this earthly life the full measure of the glory of his own station should remain concealed from the eyes of such a believer." "If the veil be lifted, and the full glory of the station of those who have turned wholly towards God, and in their love for Him renounced the world, be made manifest, the entire creation would be dumbfounded."

110   *"Verily I say! No one hath apprehended the root of this Cause. It is incumbent upon everyone, in this day, to perceive with the eye of God, and to hearken with His ear. Whoso beholdeth Me with an eye besides Mine own will never be able to know Me. None among the Manifestations of old, except to a prescribed degree, hath ever completely apprehended the nature of this Revelation." "I testify before God to the greatness, the inconceivable greatness of this Revelation. Again and again have We, in most of Our Tablets, borne witness to this truth, that mankind may be roused from its heedlessness." "How great is the Cause, how staggering the weight of its Message!" "In this most mighty Revelation all the Dispensations of the past have attained their highest, their final consummation." "That which hath been made manifest in this preeminent, this most exalted Revelation, stands unparalleled in the annals of the past, nor will future ages witness its like." "The purpose underlying all creation is the revelation of this most sublime, this most holy Day, the Day known as the Day of God, in His Books and Scriptures—the Day which all the Prophets, and the Chosen Ones, and the holy ones, have wished to witness." "The highest essence and most perfect expression of whatsoever the peoples of old have either said or written hath, through this most potent Revelation, been sent down from the heaven of the Will of the All-Possessing, the Ever-Abiding God." "This is the Day in which God's most excellent favors have been poured*

out upon men, the Day in which His most mighty grace hath been infused into all created things." "This is the Day whereon the Ocean of God's mercy hath been manifested unto men, the Day in which the Daystar of His loving-kindness hath shed its radiance upon them, the Day in which the clouds of His bountiful favor have overshadowed the whole of mankind." "By the righteousness of Mine own Self! Great, immeasurably great is this Cause! Mighty, inconceivably mighty is this Day!" "Every Prophet hath announced the coming of this Day, and every Messenger hath groaned in His yearning for this Revelation—a revelation which, no sooner had it been revealed than all created things cried out saying, 'The earth is God's, the Most Exalted, the Most Great!'" "The Day of the Promise is come, and He Who is the Promised One loudly proclaimeth before all who are in heaven and all who are on earth, 'Verily there is none other God but He, the Help in Peril, the Self-Subsisting!' I swear by God! That which had been enshrined from eternity in the knowledge of God, the Knower of the seen and unseen, is revealed. Happy is the eye that seeth, and the face that turneth towards, the Countenance of God, the Lord of all being." "Great indeed is this Day! The allusions made to it in all the sacred Scriptures as the Day of God attest its greatness. The soul of every Prophet of God, of every Divine Messenger, hath thirsted for this wondrous Day. All the divers kindreds of the earth have, likewise, yearned to attain it." "This Day *a door is open wider than both heaven and earth. The eye of the mercy of Him Who is the Desire of the worlds is turned towards all men. An act, however infinitesimal, is, when viewed in the mirror of the knowledge of God, mightier than a mountain. Every drop proffered in His path is as the sea in that mirror. For this is the Day which the one true God, glorified be He, hath announced in all His Books, unto His Prophets and His Messengers." "This is a Revelation, under which, if a man shed for its sake one drop of blood, myriads of oceans will be his recompense." "A fleeting moment, in this Day, excelleth centuries of a bygone age. . . . Neither sun nor moon hath witnessed a day such as this Day." "This is the Day whereon the unseen world crieth out, 'Great is thy blessedness, O earth, for thou hast been made the footstool of thy God, and been chosen as the seat of His mighty throne.'" "The world of being shineth, in this Day, with the resplendency of this Divine Revelation. All created things extol its saving grace, and sing its praises. The universe is wrapt in an ecstasy of joy and gladness. The Scriptures of past Dispensations celebrate the great Jubilee that must needs greet this most great Day of God. Well is it with him that hath lived to see this Day, and hath recognized its station." "This Day a different Sun hath arisen, and a different Heaven hath been adorned with its stars and its planets. The world is another world, and the Cause another Cause." "This is the Day which past ages and centuries can never* rival. Know this, and be not of the ignorant." "This is the Day whereon human ears have been privileged to hear what He Who conversed with God [Moses] heard upon Sinai, what He Who is the Friend of God [Muḥammad] heard when lifted up towards Him, what He Who is the Spirit of God [Jesus] heard as He ascended unto Him, the Help in Peril, the Self-Subsisting." "This Day is God's Day, and this Cause His Cause. Happy is he who hath renounced this world, and clung to Him Who is the Dayspring of God's Revelation." "This is the King of Days, the Day that hath seen the coming of the Best Beloved, He Who through all eternity hath been acclaimed the Desire of the World." "This is the Chief of all days and the King thereof. Great is the blessedness of him who hath attained, through the sweet savor of these days, unto everlasting life, and who, with the most great steadfastness, hath arisen to aid the Cause of Him Who is the King of Names. Such a man is as the eye to the body of mankind." "Peerless is this Day, for it is as the eye to past ages and centuries, and as a light unto the darkness of the times." "This Day is different from other days, and this Cause different from other causes. Entreat ye the one true God that He may deprive not the eyes of men from beholding His signs, nor their ears from hearkening unto the shrill voice of the Pen of Glory." "These days are God's days, a moment of which ages and centuries can never rival. An atom, in these days, is as the sun, a drop as the ocean. One single breath exhaled in the love *of God and for His service is written down by the Pen of Glory as a princely deed. Were the virtues of this Day to be recounted, all would be thunderstruck, except those whom thy Lord hath exempted." "By the righteousness of God! These are the days in which God hath proved the hearts of the entire company of His Messengers and Prophets, and beyond them those that stand guard over His sacred and inviolable Sanctuary, the inmates of the celestial Pavilion and dwellers of the Tabernacle of Glory." "Should the greatness of this Day be revealed in its fullness, every man would forsake a myriad lives in his longing to partake, though it be for one moment, of its great glory—how much more this world and its corruptible treasures!" "God the true One is My Witness! This is the Day whereon it is incumbent upon everyone that seeth to behold, and every ear that hearkeneth to hear, and every heart that understandeth to perceive, and every tongue that speaketh to proclaim unto all who are in heaven and on earth, this holy, this exalted, and all-highest Name." "Say, O men! This is a matchless Day. Matchless must, likewise, be the tongue that celebrateth the praise of the Desire of all nations, and matchless the deed that aspireth to be acceptable in His sight. The whole human race hath longed for this Day, that perchance it may fulfill that which well beseemeth its station and is worthy of its destiny."*

111   *"Through the movement of Our Pen of Glory We have, at the bidding of the Omnipotent Ordainer, breathed a*

new life into every human frame, and instilled into every word a fresh potency. All created things proclaim the evidences of this worldwide regeneration." "O people! I swear by the one true God! This is the Ocean out of which all Seas have proceeded, and with which every one of them will ultimately be united. From Him all the Suns have been generated, and unto Him they will all return. Through His potency the Trees of Divine Revelation have yielded their fruits, every one of which hath been sent down in the form of a Prophet, bearing a Message to God's creatures in each of the worlds whose number God, alone, in His all-encompassing knowledge, can reckon. This He hath accomplished through the agency of but one Letter of His Word, revealed by His Pen—a Pen moved by His directing Finger—His Finger itself sustained by the power of God's Truth." "By the righteousness of the one true God! If one speck of a jewel be lost and buried beneath a mountain of stones, and lie hidden beyond the seven seas, the Hand of Omnipotence would assuredly reveal it in this Day, pure and cleansed from dross." "Every single letter proceeding from Our mouth is endowed with such regenerative power as to enable it to bring into existence a new creation—a creation the magnitude of which is inscrutable to all save God. He verily hath knowledge of all things." "It is in Our power, should We wish it, to enable a speck of floating dust to generate, in less than the twinkling of an eye, suns of infinite, of unimaginable splen-

dor, to cause a dewdrop to develop into vast and number-less oceans, to infuse into every letter such a force as to empower it to unfold all the knowledge of past and future ages." "We are possessed of such power which, if brought to light, will transmute the most deadly of poisons into a panacea of unfailing efficacy."

112　　"The days are approaching their end, and yet the peoples of the earth are seen sunk in grievous heedlessness, and lost in manifest error." "Great, great is the Cause! The hour is approaching when the most great convulsion will have appeared. I swear by Him Who is the Truth! It shall cause separation to afflict everyone, even those who circle around Me." "Say: O concourse of the heedless! I swear by God! The promised day is come, the day when tormenting trials will have surged above your heads, and beneath your feet, saying: 'Taste ye what your hands have wrought!'" "The time for the destruction of the world and its people hath arrived. He Who is the Pre-Existent is come, that He may bestow everlasting life, and grant eternal preservation, and confer that which is conducive to true living." "The day is approaching when its [civilization's] flame will devour the cities, when the Tongue of Grandeur will proclaim: 'The Kingdom is God's, the Almighty, the All-Praised!'" "O ye that are bereft of understanding! A severe trial pursueth you, and will suddenly overtake you. Bestir your-selves, that haply it may pass and inflict no harm upon you." "O ye peoples of the world! Know, verily, that an unforeseen calamity is following you, and that grievous retribution awaiteth you. Think not the deeds ye have committed have been blotted from My sight." "O heedless ones! Though the wonders of My mercy have encompassed all created things, both visible and invisible, and though the revelations of My grace and bounty have permeated every atom of the universe, yet the rod with which I can chastise the wicked is grievous, and the fierceness of Mine anger against them terrible." "Grieve thou not over those that have busied themselves with the things of this world, and have forgotten the remembrance of God, the Most Great. By Him Who is the Eternal Truth! The day is approaching when the wrathful anger of the Almighty will have taken hold of them. He, verily, is the Omnipotent, the All-Subduing, the Most Powerful. He shall cleanse the earth from the defilement of their corruption, and shall give it for an heritage unto such of His servants as are nigh unto Him." "Soon will the cry, 'Yea, yea, here am I, here am I' be heard from every land. For there hath never been, nor can there ever be, any other refuge to fly to for anyone." "And when the appointed hour is come, there shall suddenly appear that which shall cause the limbs of mankind to quake. Then, and only then, will the Divine Standard be unfurled, and the Nightingale of Paradise warble its melody."

"In the beginning of every Revelation adversities have 113 prevailed, which later on have been turned into great prosperity." "Say: O people of God! Beware lest the powers of the earth alarm you, or the might of the nations weaken you, or the tumult of the people of discord deter you, or the exponents of earthly glory sadden you. Be ye as a mountain in the Cause of your Lord, the Almighty, the All-Glorious, the Unconstrained." "Say: Beware, O people of Bahá, lest the strong ones of the earth rob you of your strength, or they who rule the world fill you with fear. Put your trust in God, and commit your affairs to His keeping. He, verily, will, through the power of truth, render you victorious, and He, verily, is powerful to do what He willeth, and in His grasp are the reins of omnipotent might." "I swear by My life! Nothing save that which profiteth them can befall My loved ones. To this testifieth the Pen of God, the Most Powerful, the All-Glorious, the Best Beloved." "Let not the happenings of the world sadden you. I swear by God! The sea of joy yearneth to attain your presence, for every good thing hath been created for you, and will, according to the needs of the times, be revealed unto you.' "O my servants! Sorrow not if, in these days and on this earthly plane, things contrary to your wishes have been ordained and manifested by God, for days of blissful joy, of heavenly delight, are assuredly in store for you. Worlds, holy and spiritually glorious, will be unveiled to your eyes. You are destined by Him, in this world and hereafter, to partake of their benefits, to share in their joys, and to obtain a portion of their sustaining grace. To each and every one of them you will, no doubt, attain."

"This is the day in which to speak. It is incumbent 114 upon the people of Bahá to strive, with the utmost patience and forbearance, to guide the peoples of the world to the Most Great Horizon. Every body calleth aloud for a soul. Heavenly souls must needs quicken, with the breath of the Word of God, the dead bodies with a fresh spirit. Within every word a new spirit is hidden. Happy is the man that attaineth thereunto, and hath arisen to teach the Cause of Him Who is the King of Eternity." "Say: O servants! The triumph of this Cause hath depended, and will continue to depend, upon the appearance of holy souls, upon the showing forth of goodly deeds, and the revelation of words of consummate wisdom." "Center your energies in the propagation of the Faith of God. Whoso is worthy of so high a calling, let him arise and promote it. Whoso is unable, it is his duty to appoint him who will, in his stead, proclaim this Revelation, whose power hath caused the foundations of the mightiest structures to quake, every mountain to be crushed into dust, and every soul to be dumbfounded." "Let your principal concern be to rescue the fallen from the slough of impending extinction, and to help him embrace the ancient Faith of God. Your behavior towards your neighbor should be such as to manifest clearly the signs of the one true God, for ye are the first among men to be re-created by His Spirit, the first to adore and bow the knee before Him, the first to circle round His throne of glory." "O ye beloved of God! Repose not yourselves on your couches, nay, bestir yourselves as soon as ye recognize your Lord, the Creator, and hear of the things which have befallen Him, and hasten to His assistance. Unloose your tongues, and proclaim unceasingly His Cause. This shall be better for you than all the treasures of the past and of the future, if ye be of them that comprehend this truth." "I swear by Him Who is the Truth! Erelong will God adorn the beginning of the Book of Existence with the mention of His loved ones who have suffered tribulation in His path, and journeyed through the countries in His name and for His praise. Whoso hath attained their presence will glory in their meeting, and all that dwell in every land will be illumined by their memory." "Vie ye with each other in the service of God and of His Cause. This is indeed what profiteth you in this world, and in that which is to come. Your Lord, the God of Mercy, is the All-Informed, the All-Knowing. Grieve not at the things ye witness in this day. The day shall come whereon the tongues of the nations will proclaim: 'The earth is God's, the Almighty, the Single, the Incomparable, the All-Knowing!'" "Blessed is the spot, and the house, and the place, and the city, and the heart, and the mountain, and the refuge, and the cave, and the valley, and the land, and the sea, and the island, and the meadow where mention of God hath been made, and His praise glorified." "The

movement itself from place to place, when undertaken for
the sake of God, hath always exerted, and can now exert,
its influence in the world. In the Books of old the station
of them that have voyaged far and near in order to guide
the servants of God hath been set forth and written down."
"I swear by God! So great are the things ordained for the
steadfast that were they, so much as the eye of a needle, to
be disclosed, all who are in heaven and on earth would be
dumbfounded, except such as God, the Lord of all worlds,
hath willed to exempt." "I swear by God! That which hath
been destined for him who aideth My Cause excelleth the
treasures of the earth." "Whoso openeth his lips in this
day, and maketh mention of the name of his Lord, the
hosts of Divine inspiration shall descend upon him from
the heaven of My name, the All-Knowing, the All-Wise.
On him shall also descend the Concourse on high, each
bearing aloft a chalice of pure light. Thus hath it been
foreordained in the realm of God's Revelation, by the behest of Him Who is the All-Glorious, the Most Powerful."
"By the righteousness of Him Who, in this day, crieth
within the inmost heart of all created things, 'God, there
is none other God besides Me!' If any man were to arise to
defend, in his writings, the Cause of God against its as-
sailants, such a man, however inconsiderable his share,
shall be so honored in the world to come that the Concourse on high would envy his glory. No pen can depict the
loftiness of his station, neither can any tongue describe its

splendor." "Please God ye may all be strengthened to carry out that which is the Will of God, and may be graciously assisted to appreciate the rank conferred upon such of His loved ones as have arisen to serve Him and magnify His name. Upon them be the glory of God, the glory of all that is in the heavens and all that is on earth, and the glory of the inmates of the most exalted Paradise, the heaven of heavens." "O people of Bahá! That there is none to rival you is a sign of mercy. Quaff ye of the Cup of Bounty the wine of immortality, despite them that have repudiated God, the Lord of names and Maker of the heavens."

115   *"I swear by the one true God! This is the day of those who have detached themselves from all but Him, the day of those who have recognized His unity, the day whereon God createth, with the hands of His power, divine beings and imperishable essences, every one of whom will cast the world and all that is therein behind him, and will wax so steadfast in the Cause of God that every wise and understanding heart will marvel." "There lay concealed within the Holy Veil, and prepared for the service of God, a company of His chosen ones who shall be manifested unto men, who shall aid His Cause, who shall be afraid of no one, though the entire human race rise up and war against them. These are the ones who, before the gaze of the dwellers on earth and the denizens of heaven, shall arise and, shouting aloud, acclaim the name of the Almighty, and summon the children of men to the path of*

God, the All-Glorious, the All-Praised." "The day is approaching when God will have, by an act of His Will, raised up a race of men the nature of which is inscrutable to all save God, the All-Powerful, the Self-Subsisting." "He will, erelong, out of the Bosom of Power, draw forth the Hands of Ascendancy and Might—Hands who will arise to win victory for this Youth, and who will purge mankind from the defilement of the outcast and the ungodly. These Hands will gird up their loins to champion the Faith of God, and will, in My name, the Self-Subsistent, the Mighty, subdue the peoples and kindreds of the earth. They will enter the cities, and will inspire with fear the hearts of all their inhabitants. Such are the evidences of the might of God; how fearful, how vehement is His might!"

One more word in conclusion. Among some of the most momentous and thought-provoking pronouncements ever made by 'Abdu'l-Bahá, in the course of His epoch-making travels in the North American continent, are the following: *"May this American Democracy be the first nation to establish the foundation of international agreement. May it be the first nation to proclaim the unity of mankind. May it be the first to unfurl the Standard of the Most Great Peace."* And again: *"The American people are indeed worthy of being the first to build the Tabernacle of the Great Peace, and proclaim the oneness of* 116

129

mankind. . . . For America hath developed powers and capacities greater and more wonderful than other nations. . . . The American nation is equipped and empowered to accomplish that which will adorn the pages of history, to become the envy of the world, and be blest in both the East and the West for the triumph of its people. . . . The American continent gives signs and evidences of very great advancement. Its future is even more promising, for its influence and illumination are far-reaching. It will lead all nations spiritually."

117   The creative energies, mysteriously generated by the first stirrings of the embryonic World Order of Bahá'u'lláh, have, as soon as released within a nation destined to become its cradle and champion, endowed that nation with the worthiness, and invested it with the powers and capacities, and equipped it spiritually, to play the part foreshadowed in these prophetic words. The potencies which this God-given mission has infused into its people are, on the one hand, beginning to be manifested through the conscious efforts and the nationwide accomplishments, in both the teaching and administrative spheres of Bahá'í activity, of the organized community of the followers of Bahá'u'lláh in the North American continent. These same potencies, apart from, yet collateral with these efforts and accomplishments, are, on the other hand, insensibly shaping, under the impact of the world political and economic forces, the des-

tiny of that nation, and are influencing the lives and actions of both its government and its people.

To the efforts and accomplishments of those who, 118 aware of the Revelation of Bahá'u'lláh, are now laboring in that continent, to their present and future course of activity, I have, in the foregoing pages sufficiently referred. A word, if the destiny of the American people, in its entirety, is to be correctly apprehended, should now be said regarding the orientation of that nation as a whole, and the trend of the affairs of its people. For no matter how ignorant of the Source from which those directing energies proceed, and however slow and laborious the process, it is becoming increasingly evident that the nation as a whole, whether through the agency of its government or otherwise, is gravitating, under the influence of forces that it can neither comprehend nor control, towards such associations and policies, wherein, as indicated by 'Abdu'l-Bahá, her true destiny must lie. Both the community of the American believers, who are aware of that Source, and the great mass of their countrymen, who have not as yet recognized the Hand that directs their destiny, are contributing, each in its own way, to the realization of the hopes, and the fulfillment of the promises, voiced in the above-quoted words of 'Abdu'l-Bahá.

The world is moving on. Its events are unfolding 119 ominously and with bewildering rapidity. The whirlwind of its passions is swift and alarmingly violent. The New World is being insensibly drawn into its vortex. The potential storm centers of the earth are already casting their shadows upon its shores. Dangers, undreamt of and unpredictable, threaten it both from within and from without. Its governments and peoples are being gradually enmeshed in the coils of the world's recurrent crises and fierce controversies. The Atlantic and Pacific Oceans are, with every acceleration in the march of science, steadily shrinking into mere channels. The Great Republic of the West finds itself particularly and increasingly involved. Distant rumblings echo menacingly in the ebullitions of its people. On its flanks are ranged the potential storm centers of the European continent and of the Far East. On its southern horizon there looms what might conceivably develop into another center of agitation and danger. The world is contracting into a neighborhood. America, willingly or unwillingly, must face and grapple with this new situation. For purposes of national security, let alone any humanitarian motive, she must assume the obligations imposed by this newly created neighborhood. Paradoxical as it may seem, her only hope of extricating herself from the perils gathering around her is to become entangled in that very web of international association which the Hand of an inscrutable

Providence is weaving. 'Abdu'l-Bahá's counsel to a highly placed official in its government comes to mind, with peculiar appropriateness and force: You can best serve your country if you strive, in your capacity as a citizen of the world, to assist in the eventual application of the principle of federalism, underlying the government of your own country, to the relationships now existing between the peoples and nations of the world. The ideals that fired the imagination of America's tragically unappreciated President, whose high endeavors, however much nullified by a visionless generation, 'Abdu'l-Bahá, through His own pen, acclaimed as signalizing the dawn of the Most Great Peace, though now lying in the dust, bitterly reproach a heedless generation for having so cruelly abandoned them.

That the world is beset with perils, that dangers are 120 now accumulating and are actually threatening the American nation, no clear-eyed observer can possibly deny. The earth is now transformed into an armed camp. As much as fifty million men are either under arms or in reserve. No less than the sum of three billion pounds is being spent, in one year, on its armaments. The light of religion is dimmed and moral authority disintegrating. The nations of the world have, for the most part, fallen a prey to battling ideologies that threaten to disrupt the very foundations of their dearly won political unity. Agitated multitudes in these countries seethe with discontent, are armed to the teeth, are stampeded with fear, and groan beneath the yoke of tribulations engendered by political strife, racial fanaticism, national hatreds, and religious animosities. *"The winds of despair,"* Bahá'u'lláh has unmistakably affirmed, *"are, alas, blowing from every direction, and the strife that divides and afflicts the human race is daily increasing. The signs of impending convulsions and chaos can now be discerned. . . ."* *"The ills,"* 'Abdu'l-Bahá, writing as far back as two decades ago, has prophesied, *"from which the world now suffers will multiply; the gloom which envelops it will deepen. The Balkans will remain discontented. Its restlessness will increase. The vanquished Powers will continue to agitate. They will resort to every measure that may rekindle the flame of war. Movements, newly born and worldwide in their range, will exert their utmost for the advancement of their designs. The Movement of the Left will acquire great importance. Its influence will spread."* As to the American nation itself, the voice of its own President, emphatic and clear, warns his people that a possible attack upon their country has been brought infinitely closer by the development of aircraft and by other factors. Its Secretary of State, addressing at a recent Conference the assembled representatives of all the American Republics, utters no less ominous a warning. "These resurgent forces loom threateningly throughout the world—their ominous shadow falls athwart our own Hemisphere." As to its Press, the same note of warning and of alarm at an approaching danger is struck. "We must be prepared to defend ourselves both from within and without. . . . Our defensive frontier is long. It reaches from Alaska's Point Barrow to Cape Horn, and ranges the Atlantic and the Pacific. When or where Europe's and Asia's aggressors may strike at us no one can say. It could be anywhere, any time. . . . We have no option save to go armed ourselves. . . . We must mount vigilant guard over the Western Hemisphere."

The distance that the American nation has traveled 121 since its formal and categoric repudiation of the Wilsonian ideal, the changes that have unexpectedly overtaken it in recent years, the direction in which world events are moving, with their inevitable impact on the policies and the economy of that nation, are to every Bahá'í observer, viewing the developments in the international situation, in the light of the prophecies of both Bahá'u'lláh and 'Abdu'l-Bahá, most significant, and highly instructive and encouraging. To trace the exact course which, in these troubled times and pregnant years, this nation will follow would be impossible. We can only, judging from the direction its affairs are now taking, anticipate the course she will most likely choose to pursue in her relationships with both the Republics of America and the countries of the remaining continents.

122   A closer association with these Republics, on the one hand, and an increased participation, in varying degrees, on the other, in the affairs of the whole world, as a result of recurrent international crises, appear as the most likely developments which the future has in store for that country. Delays must inevitably arise, setbacks must be suffered, in the course of that country's evolution towards its ultimate destiny. Nothing, however, can alter eventually that course, ordained for it by the unerring pen of 'Abdu'l-Bahá. Its federal unity having already been achieved and its internal institutions consolidated—a stage that marked its coming of age as a political entity—its further evolution, as a member of the family of nations, must, under circumstances that cannot at present be visualized, steadily continue. Such an evolution must persist until such time when that nation will, through the active and decisive part it will have played in the organization and the peaceful settlement of the affairs of mankind, have attained the plenitude of its powers and functions as an outstanding member, and component part, of a federated world.

The immediate future must, as a result of this steady, this gradual, and inevitable absorption in the manifold perplexities and problems afflicting humanity, be dark and oppressive for that nation. The world-shaking ordeal which Bahá'u'lláh, as quoted in the foregoing pages, has so graphically prophesied, may find it swept, to an unprecedented degree, into its vortex. Out of it it will probably emerge, unlike its reactions to the last world conflict, consciously determined to seize its opportunity, to bring the full weight of its influence to bear upon the gigantic problems that such an ordeal must leave in its wake, and to exorcise forever, in conjunction with its sister nations of both the East and the West, the greatest curse which, from time immemorial, has afflicted and degraded the human race. 123

Then, and only then, will the American nation, molded and purified in the crucible of a common war, inured to its rigors, and disciplined by its lessons, be in a position to raise its voice in the councils of the nations, itself lay the cornerstone of a universal and enduring peace, proclaim the solidarity, the unity, and maturity of mankind, and assist in the establishment of the promised reign of righteousness on earth. Then, and only then, will the American nation, while the community of the American believers within its heart is consummating its divinely appointed mission, be able 124 to fulfill the unspeakably glorious destiny ordained for it by the Almighty, and immortally enshrined in the writings of 'Abdu'l-Bahá. Then, and only then, will the American nation accomplish *"that which will adorn the pages of history,"* *"become the envy of the world and be blest in both the East and the West."*

SHOGHI

December 25, 1938

INDEX

angels, 87
assistance from Almighty, 82, 89
Bahá'í Holy Places preserved, 9
Bahá'u'lláh assures Divine, 114
Concourse on high, 88, 114
God will assist pioneers, 82
hosts of Divine Inspiration, 88, 114
Invisible Hosts, 27
Providence, 3, 12
Puritanism, 50

Qualities, spiritual. *See* Character
[Queen Marie of Rumania]. *See* [Marie, Queen of Rumania]
Qur'án, 69, 75
mysteries of, not unraveled in some American states, 83
quotations from
one grain will bring forth seven sheaves, 82

Race of men, incomparable in character, will be raised up, 48,
115
Racism, 32, 51–58
'Abdu'l-Bahá's comments on, 56, 81
'Abdu'l-Bahá's example concerning, should be followed, 52
all colors are acceptable to God, 56
Bahá'u'lláh's utterances concerning, 55
diversity should be cause of love and harmony, 56
eating into vitals of society, 38
enmity between races may end in bloodshed, 56
freedom from prejudice, 36, 38
importance of overcoming prejudice, 51
most challenging issue, 51
obligation of both races in resolving, 51, 57–58
Negroes, 58
whites, 58